Model Essays 2

ncester Colle

A Practical Guide to Essay-writing for Religious
Studies A level, with Marked Examples and
Exercises

By Peter Baron

Cirencester College, GL7 1XA
Telephone: 01285 640994

Published by Active Education

www.peped.org

First published in 2019

ISBN: 9781091762657

Cartoons used with permission © Becky Dyer

Exam questions from June 2018 OCR papers © OCR

Links, reviews, news and revision materials available on www.peped.org

The PEPED website allows students and teachers to explore Philosophy of Religion, Ethics and Christian Thought through handouts, film-clips, presentations, case studies, extracts, games and academic articles.

Pitched just right, and so much more than a text book, here is a place to engage with critical reflection whatever your level. Additional marked student essays are also posted.

Acknowledgements

My thanks to my colleague Andrew Capone who marked four of the Philosophy of Religion answers.

Contents

Introduction

This book contains nineteen essays written on subjects in the OCR H573 specification, which include at least one from each section for the papers Philosophy of Religion, Ethics and Christian Thought. Each essay is written in 40 minutes by a student. The comments are either my own or those of my colleague Andrew Capone. The essays have been graded as follows: there are eight A* answers (several with full marks), four A grade answers, three B grade and four grade C.

My opening chapter discusses Level 6, the highest level of assessment which we need to aim for to be certain of A* or A grade. The weighting within the marks awarded has altered in the new specification, so that a maximum of 16 marks are awarded for knowledge and understanding (so-called AO1 criteria) and 24 marks for analysis and evaluation (AO2 criteria). I'm not sure many students understand what AO2 writing involves.

The examiners' report published on the first full GCE results of June 2018 indicated that many students' essays showed inadequate evidence of AO2 criteria being met. These answers were too full of description (knowledge) and were thin on analysis. So I try to explain in this book what analytical writing entails. I also give an exercise at the end of each essay which involves rewriting part of the essay if it is deficient in AO2 skills, or which identifies a further skill to develop perhaps with another question. I really believe that if you do these exercises you will find yourself improving.

How To Write for Level 6

In this new volume of GCE A level Religious Studies essays, candidate essays (all written under exam conditions) have been subject to deep marking by expert teachers. But this book has an additional objective. Where the previous volume explained the basis on which a mark, corresponding to one of the six levels of assessment, is awarded by an examiner, this volume goes one step further. In this volume I provide much more detailed guidance on what the key marking criteria actually mean, and provide suggestions on exercises after each essay on how to build your essay-writing skills step by step. It is hoped thereby that you can more easily understand how to write a full mark answer.

The specification launched in 2016 added a new level of assessment – level 6. So where the old specification (and the present AS specification) had only five levels, the new specification added a sixth, upper level. This created a debate among teachers: when teachers marked according to the levels they found that their students (unsurprisingly perhaps) were often achieving one level lower on average than under the old specification. They wondered whether students grades would be correspondingly lower.

What actually happened was that marks (what are called 'raw marks') were moderated up in the first full exam of June 2018, and so students generally achieved grades very similar to grades they would have achieved had there been no sixth level.

If this upwards moderation continues, I think it has an interesting consequence. If we can really understand how to hit level 6, then we will be much more likely to achieve an A* as our relative superiority will be rewarded by this upward moderation.

So we could describe the purpose of this book as a ' guide to hitting level 6'. I will begin by unpacking in full detail what the six levels are attempting to assess, illustrating were appropriate with insights from the first examiners' reports, for the June 2018 papers.

AO1 (16 marks) Knowledge & Understanding

A01 criteria seek to assess what we know and how well we understand it. To achieve level 6 we need to show excellent knowledge and understanding of the (rather general) outline of knowledge provided by the specification. Unfortunately, it's not quite as simple as 'just following the specification' for three reasons.

1. **Interpretation** of the specification is necessary as the specification is like a piece of lace – it is full of holes that need to be filled in by either you, your teacher or the textbook. Textbooks take a particular line on the rather generalised specification with the danger that (as the examiner's report notes with disapproval) students may take a conservative, textbook-orientated approach to their answers. If you want to achieve level 6, then there is an argument for throwing your textbook away (radical thought) and just building from the specification outwards, broadening, deepening and making philosophical synoptic links across

the papers as you go. Of course, this will take the formation of a level 6 virtue – moral courage – courage of your own philosophical skills and curiosity. The examiner pointed out how few students showed evidence of their own research in the 2018 paper – surely this is a big hint about the need for a change in approach.

2. **Synoptic links** are discussed in the specification on page 100-101 (at the back of a very long document). But the detail of knowledge required for each paper makes no mention of synoptic links. The synoptic links are credited – but you are going to have to work them out for yourself. There is a bias here of course toward the sort of teaching that encourages imaginative links both between the three papers (for example, Kant's noumena to Plato's Forms) and with popular culture (for example, in how secularism and pluralism work out in popular culture in the way the Archbishop of Canterbury is criticised by the secular press whenever he strays onto what the press thinks of as 'political' areas).

3. **Understanding** is different from knowledge. Knowledge tends to be descriptive – "Plato argues for a Form of the Good". Understanding has a deeper element of explanation and even illustration to it: "Plato argues for a Form of the Good which reflects itself in experienced reality as shadows reflect on the wall of a cave, because he believed that some absolute, unchangeable reality had to lie behind the appearances of things". Of course we can add another 'because' if we like – adding layers of understanding which move us up the levels – in answer to the question 'why did Plato need a Form of the Good at all?'. Notice there is no evaluation here because I am not explaining what may be wrong or

weak about this view – I am just providing another layer of understanding and insight. I am simply digging deeper into the mind of Plato.

Mistake 1: I may be tempted to spew forth knowledge as a kind of repetitive list taken from a textbook and in so doing I demonstrate little understanding and insight. Instead I should develop the moral courage to do my own research, work out my own insights and associations, and layer my understanding so it goes deep, right down into the core of the philosophical issue.

The AO1 descriptors at level 6 require "an excellent attempt to address the question showing understanding and engagement with the material; excellent ability to select and deploy relevant information. Extensive range of scholarly views, academic approaches, and/or sources of wisdom and authority are used to demonstrate knowledge and understanding" (2016 OCR GCE Specification Assessment Criteria).

Let's separate these elements so that at the end of the chapter we can produce a checklist.

• Excellent **understanding** – I have already mentioned that knowledge and understanding are not the same thing. However, understanding presupposes knowledge, so I would list the following aspects of knowledge as a foundation for good understanding.

-Knowledge of relevant **key terms** (sometimes called 'technical vocabulary'). I have listed and defined all the key terms you will need at the end of this book as an appendix for you to learn. The more nuanced we can make our definitions, the better. There are more here than actually listed in the specification itself.

-Knowledge of the background in terms of the **worldview** (not the details of where a philosopher lived, what he or she ate for breakfast and other extraneous information). The worldview also provides us with insight into **assumptions** the philosopher or author makes – for example, Aristotle assumes slaves are inferior and less intelligent caste of human being – and later we can use this knowledge as part of our evaluation.

-Knowledge of the **structure of thought** underpinning a philosopher/author's argument. You can work out your own or refer to the peped study guides which teach by structures of thought. A structure of thought works from assumption through steps of an argument (which may or not be logical) to conclusion. For example, utilitarians assume (but clearly cannot prove) that 'pleasure is the only intrinsic good'.

• Excellent **engagement** – engagement operates in two directions – engagement with the **specification** (so we know in general terms what is required of us) and engagement with the **question** in front of us. The 2018 examiner's report highlighted again how often students fail to discuss, unpack and thoroughly deal with the question in front of them, (preferring to make up their own question or reproduce a learnt answer to an essay they'd done before). I think many students need their brains retuning as this is the easiest way to fall off the higher levels.

• Excellent **selection** of material – questions usually require narrowing down so that an answer proceeds in a straight line within the time constraint of forty minutes. To reach level 6 we need to impose our own discipline on the question which requires selection and identification of the key **issues** which lurk as a kind of sub-agenda underneath the question, key **philosophers** or scholarly views (see below) and key **illustrative examples**. There needs to be a balance here. Many students try to do too much in an answer and end up doing very little successfully.

• Excellent **deployment** of material – I think this point has been covered by many of the previous points. Deployment implies a **strategy** and a strategy needs a plan. We need to send five minutes sketching our structure of thought and providing at least a **five paragraph structure** to our answer before we start writing.

• Excellent range of **scholarly views** - a futile debate has raged among teachers about how many scholars we need to mention to gain level 6. The strict answer is 'none or several but definitely not too many'. We are **required** only to demonstrate scholarly views and not to list scholars. So it is technically possible (though perhaps risky) to mention no scholars by name at all. After all, the rather generalised specification fails to mention a single utilitarian philosopher in the knowledge section of Ethics (H573/2). Again, it depends on the question set exactly what a rigorous answer will require. I suggest on the utilitarian point, we would be unwise not to engage with the utilitarianism of Bentham and Mill even if the specification doesn't require us to (we could take Singer or Sidgwick).

• Or **academic approaches** – many answers will require us to set up a tension between two or more approaches. For example, the section on Religious Language (H573/1) has a philosophical tension between the empiricist view of reality (Hume, Ayer) and a metaphysical view of reality (allowable, for example, in the thinking of Wittgenstein). We can line up these academic approaches as a tensive contrast without actually naming anyone.

• Or **sources of wisdom** and authority – we give texts authority, the authority doesn't reside in the text itself. For example, **inerrantists** give the Bible a kind of literal and absolute authority on issues such as homosexuality (Ethics – sexual ethics) and the status of women (Christian Thought – feminism), which crucially controls the kind of Christian Ethics that results (Christian Thought – Christian Moral Principles).

AO2 Criteria (24 marks) - Analysis, Evaluation & Application

A02 marks account for up to 24 marks of the total of 40 - over half the marks awarded. In practice the split between AO1 and AO2 is more like an overlapping Venn diagram because it is impossible to demonstrate understanding in the way I have explained above without using some elements of analysis. Let's explore these three words to try and unpack what they mean exactly.

Analysis implies the skill of sequencing ideas in the way I described earlier in unpacking a structure of thought. If we are to do philosophical analysis, it is characterised by clarity of thought where every step of an argument is made crystal clear. I explained this earlier in terms of breaking a viewpoint down into **structures of thought** that emerge from a worldview, for example, the Enlightenment worldview that enthrones a priori and a posteriori reason above intuition and metaphysics, through steps in the logic of the argument, to a conclusion.

Evaluation is best done step by step at each stage rather than tacked on as an afterthought. Notice that this can be done in a number of ways. One way is to criticise the structure of thought as it progresses. Perhaps it's best to illustrate this using an example below - that of utilitarian ethics, to bring out the difference between analysis and evaluation but also to show how evaluation emerges from the analysis.

Utilitarianism	Analysis	Evaluation
Assumption	There is one intrinsic good - pleasure	This cannot be proved and is doubtful as there appear to be many intrinsic goods, such as duty in Kantian ethics or agape love in situation ethics.
Logical step	We can maximise this value by making a calculation	Practically difficult as we cannot foresee consequences and we will need the wisdom of experience to assess them.
Conclusion	Goodness is best served by focusing on happiness via consequences linked to a balance of pleasure over pain.	Happiness is not an end in itself but a by-product of other things such as pursuing a hobby.

Utilitarianism	Analysis	Evaluation
	Analysis explains and justifies linkages in an argument.	Evaluation criticises and weighs up and if necessary criticises the stages of analysis.

The examiner's report 2018 again pointed out (as happens every year) that simply contrasting one philosophical viewpoint with another, and then stating that you prefer one viewpoint, is not proper evaluation. We need to provide our own judgement with clear reasons why we hold to a particular evaluation - and to justify it. As we look at the real examples in this book it should become clearer how this is done, and also, when it is not being done well. My exercises will then help you practise a method for improving evaluation.

Illustration   implies using examples to demonstrate and add clarity to your analysis. Illustrations need to be brief, and can come from anywhere (preferably not the textbook illustration as these become rather hackneyed and don't show original research). For example, films, novels, TV documentaries, soaps, art, poetry, paintings, history and present events described in newspapers all provide excellent resources and confirm that philosophy, its problems, dilemmas, challenges, is all around us.

Studying this subject is a way of opening our eyes to see, and also developing the moral courage to engage with what we discover.

Mistake 2: I may be tempted to produce lists of strengths, weaknesses, points and counter-points, or authors for and against. This can produce weak or non-existent evaluation. We need to practise writing philosophically -

which means evaluating the deeper structures of thinking at every level. Evaluation happens within and during analysis - the two are interwoven.

Descriptors at AO2 require "an **excellent** demonstration of analysis and evaluation in response to the question. Confident and insightful critical analysis and detailed evaluation of the issue. Views skilfully and clearly stated, coherently developed and justified. Excellent line of reasoning, well-developed and sustained, which is coherent, relevant and logically structured." (2016 assessment criteria).

- **Excellent analysis** implies that linkages are properly made and fully explained. One test for this is how many analytical words and phrases are used in the essay to connect ideas. I have produced my own checklist of analytical words and phrases which you will find at the back of the book. A word of warning though: these need to be used correctly. For example, the word 'because' provides reasons for a prior assertion. The word 'furthermore' implies you are about to push a previous point even further with an additional point. The word 'however' signals a contrasting point, and the word 'consequently' that something follows from what you've just said.

- **Excellent evaluation** includes critical analysis (see below) and if we refer back to the example from utilitarian ethics in the table on the preceding page, evaluation is best done at every stage of an argument rather than tacked on at the end. It's possible to come to a qualified conclusion - saying in effect that the weakness in the assumption does not completely destroy the conclusion. Utilitarians assume there is one intrinsic good, pleasure, but this doesn't entirely destroy the argument that happiness may be the best value to maximise in ethical thinking. For example, we could simply prise happiness away from an obsession with pleasure and argue, as Mill does later in his essay on utilitarianism, that happiness is a richer concept than pleasure, including such things as long term goals, the formation of character, and embracing the idea of struggle.

- **Response to the question** will involve unpacking the question and the issues implied by the question in the opening paragraph. Imagine I have a question 'meta-ethics is more useful than normative ethics'. Not only dow e need to unpack the terms 'meta-ethics' and 'normative ethics' (which might be difficult if my knowledge of key terms is shaky), but I also need to fully discuss and take a line on the phrase 'more useful than'. More useful to whom? Meta-ethics explores the foundations of ethics (the naturalism debate) and the meaning of ethical terms. So if we want to discover whether the whole naturalistic basis of many ethical theories is weak, then meta-ethics is more useful. If by contrast we wish to have guidance on how to decide a tricky issue over euthanasia or business ethics, then we ill require a normative theory to do this - meta-ethics makes no claim to resolve moral dilemmas and is useless for this purpose.

- **Confident and insightful** analysis implies a certain boldness in the presentation of a thesis (a thesis is a one sentence summary answer to the question set). I am intrigued by the word 'insightful' as many students don't seem to be aware that they are credited for insights. For

13

example, it is insightful to contrast Augustine's view of original sin with Aquinas' optimistic view of human nature summed up by the idea that we all possess **synderesis** - a God-given intuitive knowledge of right and wrong which biases us towards the good. It is insightful to compare this with Dawkins' view that we have developed an altruistic gene by natural selection, which causes us to leap into the river to save a drowning child. I include as a final chapter of this book a set of interesting insights you might like to research further to gain your own insights into how to raise your writing towards level 6.

- **Critical analysis** is part of evaluation. It means a style of writing that isn't overgeneralised and doesn't reach a conclusion ahead of a full weighing up of the steps needed to reach that conclusion. Interestingly there are often paradoxes (apparent contradictions) within a viewpoint which can be exposed and explored. You can find a paradox in virtually any philosophical view if you probe a bit more deeply.

- **Clarity** is part of excellence in both analysis and evaluation. It implies that every step of a line of reasoning is crystal clear, and any technical terms are either explained or are crystal clear in the context of sentence. There's a difference between sounding clever and being clever. The best essays in this collection manage to be both clever and clear.

- **Coherent development and justification** is part of excellence in both analysis and evaluation because an argument (or a thesis) can only be fully justified if its weaknesses and flaws are exposed. Truth needs to be tested. Linkages need to be established. Your essay needs to 'hang together' with knowledge ruthlessly pruned for relevance to your central point. Often the issue is not how much we know (though it is true some students are over-selective with their revision and so can only answer two out of the three questions), but how disciplined we are in marshalling knowledge towards the end of rigorous analysis.

- **Line of reasoning developed and sustained** is part of excellence in analysis. It implies a purpose to the essay which proceeds by clear and well argued steps. This suggests a plan is produced before you begin - and the plan needs to be nuanced (meaning, it has some subtlety built in and isn't just a list of assertions).

- **Logical structure** is part of excellence in analysis which I've covered already in considering structures of thought. It is worth exploring some of the major fallacies in philosophy - such as the fallacy of restricting the options. When AJ Ayer follows David Hume in arguing that 'meaningful sentences are either analytic or synthetic and moral language is neither', he commits a fallacy of restricting the options which excludes the possibility of metaphysical language (about God or love, or any other metaphysical idea). It's similar to arguing 'the earth is either flat or square'. We exclude the correct answer (it's round) by definition. So religious language is neither analytic nor synthetic but language of a certain type not included by the restricted options.

Below is a checklist you can use when assessing your own essays.

Checklist	Explanation	Self-assessment
AO1 (16 marks)		
Knowledge	Key terms	
	Worldview/context	
	Structure of thought	
Engagement	Specification	
	Question set	
Understanding	Deployment of material	
	Scholarly views	
AO2 (24 marks)		
Analysis	Line of reasoning Linkages Logic	
Evaluation	Criticisms Weighing up Owning a viewpoint	
Clarity	The overall thesis is transparent. Generalisations are explained and linkages made explicit.	
Coherence	The answer hangs together with a strong line of reasoning.	
Logic	One paragraph follows from another - see linkages.	

Philosophy of Religion Essays H573/1

'It is impossible to argue for the existence of God from his attributes'. Discuss (35/40, Grade A)

Arguably, we cannot derive the existence of God from His definition due to the inherent ambiguities of the predicate, existence, and indeed the nature of the subject Himself, God. Beyond this, the definition that would be used – a supremely perfect being – deeply undermines the theological idea of an epistemological space (extolled by John Hick), which allows us to develop a more meaningful relationship with God based on faith.

Good opening paragraph which gives a very clear thesis and indicates a sensible scope for answering the question effectively - the use of Hick. The idea mentioned here (epistemological space) will require clear explanation, however, otherwise it functions only as an interesting assertion which cannot gain much credit by itself. We need a brief word about what we mean by 'attributes' to show full engagement with the question set.

This type of argument, an 'ontological argument' is an a priori, and deductive. *The idea of a deductive argument could be briefly explained here, and contrasted with inductive (teleological and cosmological) arguments.* Medieval Platonic monk Anselm produced one, which tries to show that God is 'de dicto necessary' (i.e. necessary through language). It begins with Anselm, who argues (in his 'Prosologion') that God is 'that – which – nothing – greater – can – be – conceived'. He makes the case that if we were to compare a log to a horse they might say that the horse is greater (i.e. having movement). Likewise, if they were to compare a horse to a human, they might conclude that the human is greater (i.e. having faculties of reason). Therefore, there must be some 'supreme good' which allows these comparisons to be drawn, and from which other matter confers value. This, he knows to be God (akin to Plato's 'Form of the God').

Good synoptic link here to Plato's Form of the Good. Very clear and well-illustrated examples and analysis.

From this definition in Anselm's 'Proslogion', he argues that things can either exist in the mind (in re)/continually or in the mind AND reality (in re & in intellect)/necessarily. And, as God is that – which – nothing – greater – can – be – conceived, He must therefore exist both in the mind AND in reality, for this must be better than to exist in the mind alone (and God is a supremely perfect being). In other words, by virtue of the way we define God, Anselm believes His existence to be necessary; alluding to Psalm 14 ("the fool says in his heart, there is no God").

Interesting mention of Psalm 14 - which perhaps might have been explained with one sentence more. Again, the candidate writes very clearly. Note the stylistic use of brackets to provide a succinct way of illustrating, explaining or defining.

A contemporary of Anselm, Gaunilo, responds by writing (his 'On behalf of the fool') that this allows anything to be 'thought into existence'. He imagines a perfect 'lost island', with warm seas, white sandy beaches and so on. This island could either exist in the mind, or in the mind AND reality. Since it's better to exist in the mind AND reality, this island must therefore exist in reality (i.e. being perfect). Clearly, as this island doesn't exist, the argument falls short for God too (a 'reductio ad absurdum'). However, this is one of the weaker criticisms of the ontological argument, as it doesn't make sense to think of islands necessarily. They are, by definition, dynamic landforms which shift and come into or go out of existence over millions of years. That is, they are wholly contingent.

Interesting discussion rejecting Gaunilo's argument with reasons. It doesn't much matter what you argue in an essay; it is how you present the argument that's important. Above all, this candidate avoids just making assertions.

As aforementioned, the greatest drawback of this type of argument is its assumption that existence is a predicate at all. As an existent God appears not to add anything to our understanding of Him. A well-educated Theologian and a well-educated atheist have exactly the same conceptions of God, even if there's disagreement over His existence.

The word 'predicate' needs to be explained. See the glossary of key terms at the end of this book.

This was the argument set out most notably by German Philosopher Kant, in response to a reformulation of the Ontological argument by Descartes (in brief, that a supremely perfect being must have the 'perfection' of existence'). Beyond existence appearing not to be a predicate, there's arguably no reason why we cannot believe that if such a supremely perfect being existed, He would have existence. (But, since He doesn't, He does not). For example, one can describe the perfect mermaid as being half-human, half-fish and as having existence, whilst still rejecting the concept of a perfect mermaid in its entirety.

Not many students make the correct link from Kant to Descartes as it was Descartes' formulation that Kant is rejecting. Perhaps a bit more explanation is required here of Descartes' argument.

Therefore, the problems with understanding both the nature of existence and the essence of God mean that we cannot derive the existence of God from His definition, Anselm argues, that things can either be self-evidently true in themselves, or self-evidently true in themselves and to us. Although, for them to be self-evidently true in themselves and to us, we must have complete understanding of existence and God (i.e. the predicate and the subject), which we do not. As such, one can make the case that God's definition makes His existence self-evidently true in itself but this form or argument (from definition) does not convincingly show that God's existence is self-evidently true to us.

Very good - this is a subtle point clearly made.

Contemporary Frege-Russellian also disputes existence as a predicate, instead referring to it as 'the existential quest......'

If the candidate is going to employ Frege and Russell, more needs to be said by way of explanation otherwise this doesn't add very much.

Finally, many theologians write about a 'self-limitation' of God's divine attributes, in order for Him to allow us a more genuine relationship to develop. In other words if God's existence was completely known to us by definition, we would have no choice as to whether to believe in Him or not. What makes a relationship with God valuable is the fact that we freely choose to believe in it through faith. 1 Corinthians (i.e. St Paul) refers to this ambiguity when it is written that we 'see God through a glass, darkly'. There is scant Biblical evidence to the contrary, that God's definition is completely known to us. Theologian John Hick refers to this as our 'epistemological space' (or 'knowledge gap') in which to operate.

A brief tangential allusion here to other possible attributes - but a bit late in the essay.

To conclude, we certainly cannot derive God's existence from His definition due to the problematic logic, with which He is defined and because taking this to be true would critically undermine our freedom to engage in a relationship with Him. Or, as DZ Phillips suggests, perhaps it doesn't make sense to question God's existence at all. Instead, we shall take this as the starting point for theology, in the same way that other academics of integrity have axioms on which further investigation rests (e.g. Maths, Physics, Chemistry).

Essay is let down a bit here by a rather unclear concluding paragraph. The essay shows good knowledge generally here, but moves off level 6 AO2 by a failure to discuss the question enough, and unpack the idea of 'attributes' and 'predicates' fully enough. Understanding is assumed rather than made explicit.

AO1 Level 6 14 marks

AO2 Level 5 21 marks

Overall 35/40 (89%) Grade A

Exercise: Write an opening paragraph for the exam question 'you can't prove God's existence from his attributes' that clearly demonstrates engagement with the words 'existence', 'proof' and 'attribute'. You might also introduce and explain briefly the word 'predicate' (although this is not mentioned in the title).

Exercise: Here's a different question: 'Plato's view of the world is more convincing than that of Aristotle.' Discuss. Taking this question, write a paragraph **only** unpacking the non-technical word 'convincing'. This could refer to universal necessary a priori knowledge that is unchanging, or an Aristotelean view based on requirements of empirical justification (a posteriori proofs). Why did Plato need **Forms** of the Good at all? Why does Aristotle reject the Platonic worldview? What makes one view 'more convincing' than another?

To what extent does the cosmological argument withstand the challenges presented to it. (24/40 marks, Grade C)

The cosmological argument is an argument for the existence of God, based on God's alleged ability to create the universe. Arguments generally refer to God as first cause, Prime Mover or explanation. The argument claims that all things in nature are contingent and that everything depends on a being which exists independently or necessarily, which is God.   Many people have challenged Aquinas' cosmological argument, especially Hume. I believe that the cosmological argument does not withstand the challenges very well, however, some of the challenges it does slightly, for example, the idea that causality cannot be proved, I do not think is a very strong challenge.

This is a pretty good introduction. It is clear what the candidate is setting out to do and has a fairly clear thesis statement. The candidate might have clarified what was meant by "or explanation" (line 3) as a reference to God, for example, it could have meant "sufficient reason", echoing Leibniz's argument.

One of Hume's challenges to the cosmological argument is the idea that we cannot really say God explains the universe if we cannot understand the nature of God and therefore, cannot claim to truly understand the explanation. I think this is a fairly strong criticism, because Aquinas with

23

the cosmological argument seems to take a leap of logic, you cannot come to a conclusion of something when you cannot prove or know something of what makes or includes to get to that conclusion.

This last sentence is a little unclear. Aquinas makes a point of not ascribing any attributes to God, in fact Aquinas merely comments that there needs be a first mover, and that is what God is, rather than leaping to a God with no evidence of one.

Additionally, who really understands the Big Bang theory, it does not make too much sense. *It is unclear why this opinion has been included.* However, there is evidence if the Big Bang though, whereas, there is no evidence of God. For example, the red shift and the ever expanding universe. *This is not proof of the Big Bang, it is evidence that some people believe suggests the Big Bang. There are plenty of physicists who dispute the theory of the Big Bang and prefer Inflation or Steady State.* Because there is no evidence of God, we cannot understand the nature of God and so he surely cannot be the explanation of the cause of the universe, because there is no evidence. However, there is for the Big Bang theory, so surely we do not need to find an alternative cause of the universe when the evidence and proof is already there.

The candidate has not really presented any of Hume's challenges here. Only that Aquinas does not show any understanding of God's nature, which he never intended to do, and that there is no evidence, when Aquinas' point is that motion, causation and contingency are the evidence that points to God. The candidate may not have understood Aquinas' arguments. Moreover,

Hume's challenges are not represented here, e.g. the fallacy of causation and the fallacy of composition.

However, not all of Hume's challenges are strong and the cosmological argument withstands some of them quite well. For example, Hume's challenge that there is no way to prove causality. You cannot prove that one event brings about another in any causal way. Causation is just appearance. For example, cartoon characters do not actually move, it is just a series of still images that create the illusion of motion. This seems a fairly weak challenge, because Hume is not realising that there is probably many causes not just one. *On the contrary, one of Hume's challenges was that there may be many causes. His example was that a ship is not caused by one shipwright but many shipwrights.* By saying God is the uncaused cause does not eliminate the possibility of further causes. Surely things cannot have one single cause but many that make up a cause, for example, there is not one cause of a house being built, there are many: many builders, many processes and materials put together. Additionally, causation may be appearance, but I still think causes are strong, important indications of how things come about.

The candidate has not really understood Hume's challenge. He is saying that there is no way of proving the cause of something if you only have the effect and have no experience of causes of those things. E.g. I may have experience of where babies come from because I have seen women give birth, so when I see a baby I can accurately assume that he/she was born. I have not seen universes be created so I cannot assume that this universe was created when all I have is the effect. Hume gave the example of the billiard balls. The motion in B is different from the motion in A.

However, a stronger challenge to the cosmological argument is Hume's challenge of infinite regress, that I believe the cosmological argument cannot withstand very well. Aquinas talks about the idea that infinite regress is impossible, because if all causes have previous causes then there's no cause that causes motion and change in the first place. However, Hume challenges this and believes that infinite regress is possible, take mathematics, for example. As energy and matter are interchangeable, then why can it not be seen that the universe is equivalent to energy which is eternal. Also if an infinite series is possible then there is no need for a sufficient reason.

The meaning of sufficient reason is to explain the whole series.

This in my opinion is a fairly strong challenge to the cosmological argument, however I do think this challenge has some weaknesses too and is not completely strong. This is because the Big Bang theory proves that the universe had a beginning, eliminating the idea there is an infinite number of causes, there is also evidence of the Big Bang so this makes Hume's challenge even weaker. *As previously commented, there are many who dispute the Big Bang.* However, the idea of infinite regress does seem possible, because it seems hard to believe there was one cause and point in time where the universe came into being and was caused, surely there has to be infinite causes and time, because how can there be a beginning when there is nothing to cause that beginning? *This is not a response or challenge. Avoid rhetorical questions, rather present an actual line of* reasoning. *There is nothing wrong with the idea of fixed point creation, many physicists accept it.* Some may say that would be God who could do that, but something surely would have to of caused God (*'have to HAVE caused God', not 'have to OF caused God'*) to do that in the first place, meaning if God did exist there would have to be something superior to God to cause God, but the problem is there must be something else to cause that superior being which means there is an infinite chain. *Not really, this is a typical challenge "if God caused the world, what caused God". It is a simple misunderstanding of the question. It is not that God is a link in the chain of causes, but rather that at the end of the chain there is a first cause that is itself "uncaused". Whatever and wherever that uncaused first cause is, that is what we call God.* Therefore, it seems more possible that there is no God that causes the universe but an infinite chain of causes, meaning Hume's challenge is stronger than I originally thought, meaning the cosmological argument finds it harder to withstand these challenges. *"Stronger than I originally thought" suggests that the candidate does not have a plan at the start but is working toward an answer mid essay.* Additionally, although infinite regress is hard to imagine it does not therefore, mean it is impossible, this idea was made by William Temple 'it is impossible to imagine infinite regress[but] it is not impossible to conceive it".

A fine comment here. The infinite regress challenge is a good challenge to use in this essay.

Additionally, a strong challenge to the cosmological argument is Hume's idea of experience. We have no experience of universes being made. We know about causes within the universe but this does not entitle us to move to a cause of the universe as a whole. Bertrand Russel also supports this challenge by saying that you cannot say that because a man has a mother mankind has a mother, it is too much of a leap. These views link to the Fallacy of Composition, what it true of the part does not mean it is true of the whole. I think this challenge is a very strong one, because Aquinas in so many parts of the cosmological argument takes too many leaps and quickly assumes things without thinking it through thoroughly. _This is not how Aquinas commits this fallacy._ There is evidence of how the universe was made, for example, the Big Bang with the red shift, however, we have not experienced it being made at the beginning. Therefore, we cannot say that God definitely caused the universe, because we were not there too witness that happening.

Some good knowledge here fairly well debated.

Although, many of Hume's challenges have some slight weaknesses, overall I think they are very strong making the cosmological argument a very weak one, not withstanding the challenges very well. I especially think the challenge of experience is very strong.

A simple conclusion, not a surprise as the candidate sticks to the thesis statement fairly well throughout the essay.

AO1 Level 4 (9 marks): *Some good knowledge of the challenges Hume presents, but a lot of the essay shows a weak understanding of Aquinas' three Ways themselves.*

AO2 (15 marks): *Some debate and attempt to analyse the arguments, however, the first paragraph in the essay proper really does not answer the question or show understanding of Hume's challenges.*

Overall: 24/40 C Grade

Exercise: Rewrite the following paragraph to explain accurately and fully Hume's objections to the cosmological argument, taking the marker's comments and suggestions into account.

"However, not all of Hume's challenges are strong and the cosmological argument withstand some of them quite well. For example, Hume's challenge of there is no way to prove causality. You cannot prove that one event brings about another in any causal way. Causation is just appearance. For example, cartoon characters do not actually move, it is just a series of still images that create the illusion of motion. This seems a fairly weak challenge, because Hume is not realising that there is probably many causes not just one. By saying God is the uncaused cause does not eliminate the possibility of further causes. Surely things cannot have one single cause but many that make up a cause, for example, there is not one cause of a house being built, there are many: many builders, many processes and materials put together. Additionally, causation may be appearance, but I still think causes are strong, important indications of how things come about."

'There is no design in the universe'. Discuss. (34/40 marks, Grade A)

Teleological arguments for the existence of God aim to show design qua purpose or qua regularity. Paley, Aquinas, Swinburne, Tennant and Behe have produced arguments based on the appearance of design in the universe indicating a designer which they believe is God. If we just 'see' the universe as looking designed but it is not actually, then all teleological arguments for the existence of God fail. I do not believe the universe was designed by an external, intelligent being, I believe it came about by chance, naturally, which I think the scholars mentioned above do not consider enough, they are too distracted by what they 'see' and automatically believe this is 'design'. Just because something is complex and ordered is not sufficient evidence of 'design', why couldn't something complex come about by chance? However, my opinion is not completely definite, some ideas of design do question my opinion, for example Behe's example of the mousetrap. Hume, Mill and Darwin gave different arguments of how the universe was made, which agree with my views much more.

This introduction is developed and clearly explains where the essay will go. Avoid rhetorical questions in an essay, unless you are fully interrogating the question. Instead show a line of reasoning. Notice the full range of scholars mentioned here.

Claims made for design in the universe are a posteriori. These include Paley's qua purpose argument, qua purpose is in the sense that the universe was designed to fulfil a purpose and qua regularity is in the sense that the universe behaves according to some order. In Natural Theology Paley compared the complexity of the universe with a watch, he stated that it was easy to know if something was naturally made " I could easily account for its existence". You also know if something is man-made, because of its complexity and intricate nature, where he uses the watch as an example "I could not account for it in that natural way… reveals an array of intricate, beautifully made cogs…", he therefore says that there has to be a "watch maker", because it could not come about by chance, so the universe must also have a designer because of how complex it is as well, which must be God. Paley believes so strongly about this, because using our inference we can tell the difference between man-made and natural things, it is obvious. Secondly, because even if something is imperfect or you cannot work out the function of the machine you can still tell it has a designer because it is intricate, complex and your inference is correct. However, the effectiveness of the argument that there is design is limited by Mill's challenge of the nature of evil and his observation that there exists some things which have no evident purpose. He believes that because natural evil, for example the plague, volcanoes etc, exist then if the universe was designed it seems to be a faulty one. Therefore, if there is a designer it is morally flawed. Mill's challenge is in my opinion very effective overall in challenging the existence of God, because it makes no sense that if God existed he would create a universe with natural evil, because he is supposed to be omnibenevolent and omni-potent enough to not design natural evil, if God did design the universe then many Christian beliefs of God would be wrong. *Or atheists' understanding of God's attributes would be mistaken.* Very unlikely in my opinion but if God did exist then perhaps he designed the universe with natural evil, because if he designed the world perfectly then life would be too easy and straight forward, we would never have to go through any tough times and we need those to develop as a person, it would not be reality. Additionally, maybe because of God's omnipotence he has stopped much natural evil from happening we just do not know about it, by him not stopping it all he is acting in our best interests. *This is not a problem of evil essay.* However, I still do not believe God exists and that the universe was designed, I am just stating a point that if God did exist just because there is natural evil does not necessarily mean he is morally flawed. *Avoid chatty writing. This is a Philosophy essay, not a conversation.* Paley's teleological argument I believe has many weaknesses, for example, his analogy is flawed. You cannot compare watches to a universe, they are nothing alike, analogies should be made between two distinct things, not between something man made and natural. *Cite Hume here.* However, his analogy has some slight positives, for example, it makes comprehensible sense to us, it's simple and straightforward. However, this is no means to say I agree with Paley, additionally, what is to say there wasn't a group of watchmakers instead of one, it makes no sense to say there is one intelligent being known as God, when it could have been a group of Gods who designed the universe.

This is a good developed understanding of Paley. The challenge presented does not really live up to argument. Mill's challenge is well represented, but the challenge of analogy is not cited to Hume. Also, Dawkins' famous challenge stating that "Paley was wrong, spectacularly wrong" is missing. The theory of evolution would fit beautifully here. The paragraph is rather long, although the use of analytical words and phrases suggest an argument is being developed.

Thomas Aquinas offers a different teleological argument. His 5th Way of the Summa is influenced by Aristotle's four causes and has a teleological view that everything in the universe has a purpose. Here he is presenting an a posteriori qua purpose argument for the existence of God. He uses an arrow and an archer to state that everything aims to their telos which has intelligence or an "intelligent being" has to direct that thing. Therefore, even inanimate things seem to act towards a particular end, which to Aquinas is directed by an intelligent being, which is God. However, Hume's argument goes against this teleological theory, he states that the appearance of design might be the result of random events. This is seen in Hume's Epicurean Thesis. This is the idea that there is not a designer, instead the universe was made naturally, which I highly agree with. If there was infinite time and finite particles they would undergo every possible combination. Some of those combinations would be stable and would over time form the universe. Hume's argument is effective because he shows that the universe could have come around by chance and create complex, beautiful structures without having to be designed. They might come about rarely and remain, whereas ugly and dysfunctional structures may of died away *('may HAVE died away', not 'may OF died away')*, due to them not being complex enough to function (this is very similar to Robert Hambourger). We don't see the dysfunctional things dying away, because only the complex things may remain the in the universe, therefore, too many people believe that that is all that has been created, because that is all they 'see'. However, we do not actually know if this is order it may be chaos, as it could be our perception we impose. Hume would believe this, because you cannot assume the universe is designed just because you see patterns. 'Apparent' order is not the same as 'intended' order. In Hume's dialogues he mentioned this using 'Philo' as a critic. Additionally, I agree with Hume and disagree with Aquinas, because even if you did prove the world was designed that would not mean that we could infer that it was made by the Christian God. *Aquinas does not infer this.* Hume used an analogy of a ship to explain this point I just mentioned, he put forward that it was made by a team of shipwrights, not one solitary shipwright. Although I agree with Hume I do not think this particular criticism is a very strong one, because he believed that you cannot compare the universe to a machine and now he is comparing using a ship, it does not seem a very useful analogy. *Nice!* Secondly, if God did exist he would be omni-potent , not like a ship-maker, he could be the sole designer of the world. However, I still disagree with Aquinas, for example, using an arrow to compare to the rest of the universe, is flawed, analogies should be between two distinct things, not a whole thing and a part within it. *Aquinas was using analogy in comparing similar characteristics between things. The arrow is inanimate. The universe is (so it would seem) inanimate. That is the extent to which he is comparing them. He did a lot of work on*

analogies. Additionally, if the world was designed, that designer may have a designer, leading to an infinite regress. The all powerful designer would have to have been made by another all powerful designer, because how else would a designer come about if there was one?

Very good understanding of Aquinas here and some good use of Hume's challenges. The paragraph is rather long and contains a number of ideas that could have been split up more sequentially.

Furthermore, a significant challenge to the appearance of design in the universe comes from Darwin's evolutionary theory. Darwin's theory suggests that species develop by a process of random mutation and that the fittest survive if they adapt to their environments 'the survival of the fittest', for example the finches on the Galapagos Islands whose beaks changed over time. The rest die out and only a select few species survive, because 'Life is a struggle to exist'. This is supporting Hume's idea that 'apparent' order can come from chaos. If countless number of species have not survived, because they could not adapt, then if this represents design it seems a wasteful process. If all species have evolved from simpler species, that indicates that we were not designed as we are. If we had to adapt to environments then that shows that we were not designed fit for purpose, but rather that we are adapted to needs. This is a challenge to the qua purpose teleological argument and points to the idea that there is no designer or if there is one then it is a very faulty one, and not a omni-potent God may Christians say he is. Although I believe this theory and that the universe was not designed, this theory does not necessarily rule out design. According to Aquinas the universe was designed with order and pattern 'acting for an end', as F.R Tennant says, you could easily see that God could have used evolution in designing the universe, to create life. However, I still believe that the universe came about naturally, through evolution, I agree with Hume's theory but I do not think it is as persuasive and effective as Darwin's.

Correction: the universe cannot have come about via evolution, rather, life evolved over time within the world. The world still needs accounting for. Notice the excellent use of an analytical word 'furthermore' at the start of the paragraph.

In conclusion, to say that there is design implies there is an intelligent designer, inferring that God exists, this is supported by Paley and Aquinas. However, Hume, Mill and Darwin say they are too worried about the appearance of design and instead criticise that it is 'apparent' and not reality. I believe you cannot rule out design completely, because for example, Behe said there are things in nature that are 'irreducibly complex' parts have no function for natural selection to work unless they are together. These incredibly complex things in the universe, for example the process of blood coagulation is extremely clever, and makes you question whether there is any design in that. I still believe the universe was not designed, although those points do make me question my opinion a bit more. *If Behe is worth mentioning, mention him in the essay proper. Do not include anything new in the conclusion.* I believe the challenges to intelligent design are more persuasive than the teleological arguments. The evolutionary theory especially is a very strong argument for the universe coming about naturally, and is solid evidence against the universe being designed. For example, the finch's beaks that changed over time to adapt to their environments, indicates no design because their original beaks had to change and were not sufficient enough for their purpose in the universe.

Except for the inclusion of Behe which is out of place, a good strong conclusion summing up the thesis statement.

AO1: Level 5 (13 marks) *A lot of very good knowledge in breadth and depth. Lots of good use of scholars and quotes.*

AO2: Level 5 (18 marks) *Good argument, thesis statement clear and there is a strong line of reasoning throughout the essay. Some attempt to analyse and justify arguments presented. Paragraphing might be improved.*

Overall: 31/40 A Grade

Exercise: Turn the essay above into a plan with an eight paragraph structure, extracting the main ideas in summary form. The first paragraph should contain a thesis statement.

'The best approach to understanding religious language is through the cataphatic way.' Discuss (19/40 marks, Grade C/D)

The cataphatic way is one of numerous proposed ways to discuss God and his nature, with support coming from Christian theologian Thomas Aquinas. The cataphatic way is controversial however, with criticisms of Moses Maimonides stating it is insulting to describe God in such human language, while Dutch thinker Plantinga proposes the doctrine of fideism is the only true way to understand God.

The introduction is sound in that it identifies what the essay will cover, however, there should be a clear thesis statement identifying whether the candidate agrees or disagrees with the statement itself. Many candidates muddled up the cataphatic and anaphatic ways. This made no difference to their final level - the examiner took the term anaphatic as if it was written 'cataphatic'.

Christian theologian Thomas Aquinas supported the use of the cataphatic way, stating that while we couldn't describe God literally or directly, we could describe him through analogies. For example, when God is described as a father, we aren't literally describing God as a father but instead conveying the perfect nature of God through an analogy.

This paragraph is accurate, if asserted. Some development would help to bring this up a level.

However, the thinker Moses Maimonides argues it is insufficient to use the cataphatic way to describe God, calling it insulting to describe God with flawed human terms. Agreeing with Aquinas that we cannot describe God literally, Maimonides argues that the entirety of human language is flawed, so analogies to describe God and his nature are insufficient.

This is fairly accurate. However, it is a little more than this. Maimonides said that using positive language would result in a loss of faith. It would be good to justify this position with the example of the ship.

Maimonides' view however is not supported by the Bible, with the cataphatic way being used to describe God. For sola scriptura Christians, therefore, Maimonides' criticism is unconvincing.

An example of cataphatic way in the Bible would be advised here.

An outside observer, however, may argue that the use of the cataphatic way in the Bible is a non-sequitur to the utility of using it in religious language. For example, the apophatic way is used in various Buddhist texts to describe the nature of true reality and understanding, so to use the Bible is unappealing to anyone outside of the Abrahamic faiths.

Interesting view here, comparing with Buddhist ideas. However, remember that talking about divine reality is not the same as talking about God. Granted there is a "religious" element in both, but there is a sweeping assumption here that all Abrahamic faiths somehow use the Bible and that the Bible is all cataphatic. A lot of assertions here without justification.

The Dutch thinker Plantinga criticises both the cataphatic and apophatic way, instead offering the doctrine of fideism. Plantinga argues humanity has no way to make claims about the knowledge of God, and no amount of rationality or reason can help us understand God.

Asserted, not fully justified. Notice how short the paragraphs are, suggesting underdevelopment of the argument.

The atheist response, however, is that this is a deep appeal to faith fallacy, which asks us to stop critically thinking about the nature of God and instead blindly accept assertions about God. The thinker Christopher Hitchens may go one step further and criticise the entirety of religious language with his Hitchens' Razor – that which can be asserted without evidence can be dismissed without evidence.

This is not really answering the question. Also, in response to the Hitchens razor, the problem is that atheists that apply the Hitchens razor don't accept the evidence that is presented or accepted by religious people, so it is not that there is no evidence, it is that they don't accept it as evidence.

However, Christian thinker John Hick offers a Pascalian outlook to religious language. He argues that we should accept cataphatic statements about God because we have little to lose and much to gain by believing in these statements. Further, he argues, these statements will be verified at the end of time due to the eschatological verification principle, so the best option for the time being is to accept cataphatic statements about God's nature.

Eschatological verification was a response to the 20th Century influence of Logical Positivism. It is not particularly relevant in this essay.

In conclusion, many theologians have argued over the best way to discuss religious language. Appeals to the Bible as proof of the cataphatic way's utility could be argued as a non-sequitur by those outside of the Abrahamic faith, considering the use of the apophatic way in Buddhist texts. However, atheist thinkers like Hitchens are convincing in their criticisms of all religious language – that it breaks his razor as it is all assertions with no evidence to back up claims, with instead appeals to faith or chance replacing evidence.

AO1: 7/16

The candidate has some good knowledge and understanding; however, the material selected is not directly relevant to the question in most cases. The question is about the Cataphatic Way, which means the candidate should have discussed the two forms of analogy: analogy of proportionality and analogy of attribution, and then compared it with Tillich's symbols.

AO2: 12/24

The candidate did some good analysis and evaluation with Moses Maimonides, though, like much of the essay, this was asserted with little justification. The candidate tried to evaluate with Hitchens, Buddhist ideas and Hick, but these perspectives were often off topic. The candidate should focus on the material identified in the specification before tackling alternative perspectives on the question.

19/40 Grade C/D borderline

Exercise: The following paragraph contains a number of assertions that are not properly developed and explained. Research Plantinga and then rewrite the paragraph so that it forms a full analysis rather than a set of assertions. Make sure you fully explain 'the doctrine of fideism' so that a non-specialist can grasp your intended argument.

The Dutch thinker Plantinga criticises both the cataphatic and apophatic way, instead offering the doctrine of fideism. Plantinga argues humanity has no way to make claims about the knowledge of God, and no amount of rationality or reason can help us understand God.

Exercise: The following paragraph is underdeveloped. Rewrite it in a way that more fully brings out the main points.

However, the thinker Moses Maimonides argues it is insufficient to use the cataphatic way to describe God, calling it insulting to describe God with flawed human terms. Agreeing with Aquinas that we cannot describe God literally, Maimonides argues that the entirety of human language is flawed, so analogies to describe God and his nature are insufficient.

'Corporate religious experiences are less reliable than individual experiences'. (40/40 marks Grade A*) Discuss (OCR H573/1, June 2018)

It can be argued that corporate religious experiences are less reliable than individual religious experiences such as mystical, numinous or conversion, as they can be subject to mass hysteria. William James would agree that they are less reliable as he strongly argues that conversion experiences can be proven for validity, therefore are reliable. On the other hand, scholars such as Schleiermacher and Swinburne would argue that all religious experiences are equally reliable, as this is an extremely weak view to take as religious experiences should be taken on a case by case basis and it is dangerous to make blanket statements such as one is more reliable than the other. In fact it can be even argued that no religious experience is reliable and can be proven and explained by psychology. Therefore it is wrong to claim that corporate religious experiences are less reliable than others, as they should all be judged case by case.

Notice how easy it is to reconstruct the question from this opening paragraph, even if we didn't have the question in front of us – the sign of a potential top grade answer. The thesis is crystal clear from this paragraph - "it s wrong to claim that…".

Corporate religious experiences are those that happen to a group of people as a body. An example of a corporate religious experience is the story of Pentecost as the crowds all felt the same mighty winds and saw

43

the same fountains of fire. In addition a more recent corporate experience is the Toronto blessing, where people all felt the same euphoric sensation and experienced uncontrollable laughter. A case can be made that corporate religious experiences such as these are reliable as there is more than one person claiming that this happened, although this is an extremely weak argument, as who says they aren't all lying? This can be seen with the corporate religious experiences of six teenagers and children in Medjugorge (former Yugolsavia, June 1981), where they claimed to keep seeing the virgin Mary and she would deliver messages to them such as 'the world needs more prayer'. However, the Catholic church itself is extremely sceptical of this religious experience and warns others to be as well, therefore demonstrating that corporate experiences perhaps are less reliable. However, these explanations may have a neuropsychologcial explanation, particularly the Toronto blessing, as Michael Persinger's God helmet demonstrated that experiences can be caused by being in the presence of magnetic fields and not bought about by God. Thus demonstrating corporate religious experiences are not reliable. But this objection can be used for individual religious experiences, highlighting that all types of religious experiences are equally as reliable or unreliable as each other.

This is high quality analytical writing, typified by the sort of words I have underlined. See the appendix at the back of the book for my list (arranged by theme) of analytical words and phrases. Notice that scholarly views are discussed and examples given to illustrate - fulfilling AO1 and AO2 criteria.

Friedrich Schleiermacher takes the <u>extremely controversial</u> view that all types of religious experiences are self-authenticating therefore receive absolutely no testing to see if they are reliable or not. Thus meaning he would completely disagree with the claim that corporate religious experiences are less reliable as they are all reliable in his eyes. However, this is <u>an extremely dangerous view to take</u> as it means that those experiences which may have occurred from drugs or other influences are considered valid religious experiences, when actually they contain no religious origin at all. Furthermore, the Catholic church presents a strong critique of Schleiermacher's view stating that <u>religious experiences do need to be tested</u> in some way, perhaps against Scripture or biblical teachings, to make sure religion is not damaged by those caused by other means. <u>This adds validity to the idea</u> that different types of religious experiences are not more or less reliable than each other but the reliability should be taken on each individual experience.

I have underlined examples of evaluative comments. Notice how analysis and evaluation are woven together to back up the main thesis of the essay.

On the other hand, William James would argue that conversion experiences are perhaps more reliable than corporate religious experiences, as James argued that with conversion experiences you can see a direct change in the subject after the experience therefore meaning it can be proven to be reliable. As James wanted to take an objective account to see if conversion experiences were reliable, therefore strengthening his conclusion. In addition, James identified five main characteristics of religious experiences that we can identify in the subject.

These are: ineffability, unable to express it in our everyday language, noetic quality, containing a sense of a truth, transience, lasts a short time but effects are lasting, and passivity, so it happens outside yourself. This therefore means that James has provided a framework in which we can test people's religious experiences against. However, this does still not mean they can be 100% reliable as those experiences caused by psychological factors may also portray the same four qualities, therefore this may prove an experience has taken place even though it is not necessarily religious. However, James would argue against this and say that we can see if it was religious or not by seeing if the person now portrays characteristics of the Holy Spirit, such as listed in the Bible , 'the Holy Spirit is joy, love, peace', therefore if you can now see those characteristics in a person, which you could not before, suggests that a religious experience has taken place and it can be said to be reliable. Although James' argument that conversion is more reliable because we can observe the effects is convincing, it doesn't completely rule out any other explanations. For example, some people may be more prone to these experiences if they have had a traumatic upbringing. Therefore psychology has an answer and not James.

*A very clear argument with a strong conclusion at the end ('therefore..')
rounds off another rigorous stage of logical structure in the essay.*

Feuerbach puts forward a convincing argument to disprove the concept of religious experiences as he states that people often invent this God figure in their own minds in order to fill the gap. For example, if someone didn't have a father figure growing up they may invent a parental 'god' like figure in their heads to fill that gap. Thus weakening James' argument that conversion experiences are reliable, as people may think its God talking to them but really it's their own human nature. This therefore demonstrates that James' is wrong in claiming individual experiences are any more reliable than corporate as they are about as reliable as each other.

The scholarly views continue, in this case Feuerbach. The writer could have made a synoptic link to Freud (conscience, Ethics paper) who argues that we transpose our need for a father-figure onto God in order to reduce our anxiety - but this is a form of infantilism.

In my judgement, corporate religious experiences are not less reliable than individual ones, as it depends on the individual unique experience and you should judge its reliability solely on the experiences and not whether it is a corporate or individual one. In addition, perhaps no type of religious experience is reliable due to the psychological explanations which are now available.

Strong conclusion which echoes the thesis outlined in the opening paragraph. Noice the rigorous analysis and interwoven evaluation which continues throughout the essay. Contrast this with the rather thin and over - assertive style of the first essay. This answer was written in forty minutes under exam conditions and attained full marks. It gives us a bench-mark to aim for.

AO1 Level 6 (16 marks) *an excellent attempt to address the question showing understanding and engagement with the material; excellent ability* to select and deploy relevant information. Extensive range of scholarly views, academic approaches, and/or sources of wisdom and authority are used to demonstrate knowledge and understanding.

AO2 Level 6 (24 marks) an excellent demonstration of analysis and evaluation in response to the question. Confident and insightful critical analysis and detailed evaluation of the issue. Views skilfully and clearly stated, coherently developed and justified. Excellent line of reasoning, well-developed and sustained, which is coherent, relevant and logically structured.

Overall: 40/40 Grade A*

Exercise: if this is the opening paragraph, what is the question? We should be able to construct the exact question from the opening paragraph.

"Aristotle's theory of the four causes is an empiricist approach that does not explain how we can attain knowledge to an extent. However there are a few problems in some areas of his theory. For example, the term 'final cause' includes the idea of the Prime Mover, but this does explain some things rather than nothing. His understanding of formal cause rather than explaining nothing, is also convincing to the extent that it is in line with the common sense empiricism of John Locke in the seventeenth century, and his theory is able to solve some of the problems posed by Plato's Theory of the Forms."

Exercise: Construct a thesis statement on the following question. A thesis statement is an outline summary position which you will be seeking to establish in the bulk of the essay, and should be present, by implication at least, in your opening paragraph. The thesis statement demonstrates that you are engaging with the question and also seeking to identify the sub-agenda lurking in the question.

Evaluate whether Plato's rationalism is superior to Aristotle's empiricism in making sense of reality.

Critically assess the claim that religious language is meaningless.(40/40 marks, grade A*)

Religious discourse has been exchanged for millennia, but in recent times philosophers have come to doubt whether the language of such discourse holds any meaning whatsoever. The issue is of great salience, for if one takes religious language to be devoid of any meaning, then all discussion of God, and thus religious belief, is futile. But for the believer, the ability to understand his beliefs and communicate them to others is essential, both for his own personal faith and its propagation. Many have contributed to the quandary of religious language: from the Vienna Circle of the 1920/30s to the acclaimed philosopher Ludwig Wittgenstein.

Good general introduction but it would be better if this opening paragraph contained a thesis statement - a one sentence summary of the position the writer will take on this issue. Is religious language ultimately meaningless or not?

The philosophers of the 20th Century Vienna Circle, among whom A.J Ayer was prominent, formulated what is called the Verification Principle. By this they held that language only had meaning if it could be subject to empirical verification. *It can be also analytically meaningful as is pointed out below.* The Logical Positivists maintained that there were two types of statement: analytical and synthetic. The former is a statement that is true by definition. For example, "all bachelors are unmarried men" is an analytical statement as it contains within it the truth needed to verify it. Synthetic statements are those that are true by observation. For instance,

I may remark, "It's raining outside", but my remark only has meaning as it can be tested by sense observation. The Verificationists said that religious language was neither analytical or synthetic and thus not meaningful. When a religious believer says, "God is good" he has no empirical evidence to support this; he cannot subject the proposed goodness of God to scientific inquiry and, so, according to the Verification Principle, such a statement is meaningless. Therefore, those who follow the philosophy of the Verification Principle would agree that religious language is meaningless.

Good, clear paragraph. The statement "God is good' might also be analytically meaningful as suggested by the ontological argument.

However, the stringency of Verificationist thought has drawn many criticisms. For example, followed to its extreme, the Verification Principle would conclude that we can make no meaningful pronouncements on Julius Caesar as we cannot expose them to empirical verification given that the man is dead. Thus, any discourse on Julius Caesar is meaningless. Another example might be a psychiatric patient trying to relate his symptoms to a doctor. According to the Verification Principle, any description would be pointless as the personal, internal nature of such symptoms precludes them from the doctor's realm of experience and from empirical scrutiny. Of course, most people would reject such extreme conclusions and this leads many to reject the Verification Principle itself. A.J Ayer saw this problem and altered the principle so that it allowed for "indirect experience", but Verifications still held that religious language was meaningless. John Hick also took umbrage with the theory. He claimed that any religious claim would be verified after death: "Eschatological Verification". Therefore, we may say that the Verification Principle is a poor means to demonstrate that religious language is meaningless and that such language could still hold meaning.

Excellent evaluative paragraph bringing in a number of scholarly views to establish some flaws in the verificationist position. Note the analytical language used - words like 'however', 'thus', and 'therefore' suggest we are unpicking and contrasting points.

Recognising the stringent nature of the Verification Principle, the 20th Century philosopher Anthony Flew sought to apply the Falsification Principle to religious language. In doing this, Flew borrowed the ideas of the scientist Karl Popper – a man famously critical of Freud's evidence, or lack thereof, for his theories. Popper believed that the only meaningful and valid scientific statement is one that can be falsified. For example, the claim "Water boils at one-hundred degrees centigrade" is scientific precisely because it can be falsified. There could be a situation where water is discovered to boil at ninety-five degrees centigrade. The point is that scientific statements are open to the possibility of being falsified. In applying Popper's thought to religious language, Flew argued that religious claims were not open to being falsified. For instance, a believer may claim, "God is love" and yet be challenged by the existence of an evil like AIDS. Flew says that the believer will shift the goal posts so that his claim holds. He might retort, "God is love, but faulty human choices brought evil into the world". In this way, Flew said religious language "dies a death by a thousand qualifications". Therefore, as it is not open to the possibility of being proved wrong, falsified, many have concluded with Flew that religious language is meaningless: nothing more than claims with a string of qualifications attached.

Again this shows exceptionally clear writing and the argument and evaluation is proceeding by a very clear line of logical reasoning, pushing the answer towards level 6.

Yet, Flew's Falsification Principle has come under criticism. R.M Hare said that unfalisifiable convictions were essential to helping people find meaning in their lives. He gives the example of an undergraduate who thinks all dons are out to kill him. Even if he meets a kindly don (the possibility of falsification) he declares it a trick and holds fast to his belief. Such resolute beliefs Hare called "bliks". Insofar as bliks give meaning to people's lives and help them understand the world, they have meaning. The belief that God doesn't exist is just as much a blik as the belief that God does exists and is benevolent. Therefore, it could be argued that religious language does have meaning: maybe not an objective meaning but a sort of imputed meaning given it by the individual believer.

Here, as in previous paragraphs, we have good clear and concise use of examples to illustrate the point. Not too many words are expended developing the example which is important if the analysis is to proceed coherently and concisely.

This resonates, to a degree, with the thought of Ludwig Wittgenstein. He formulated his theory of Language Games to show that religious language has meaning to a specific group of people who "play" a specific language game. For example, I may know that a "king" is monarch. But another person's perception of a "king" is that it is a chess piece that can move one space in any direction. It is not the case that one perception of "king" is correct and the other false: both are true and meaningful to the game that is being played. In the arena of religious language, this means that language such as, "God is good and has a plan for your life", can only be understood by those who "play" the game of religion. Unless one plays that game, the language of it will seem meaningless. It might be likened to a cricketer trying to play rugby with a cricket bat. The atheist can never hope to understand the meaning of religious language, unless he is religious and takes up the game of religion. Therefore, Wittgenstein was able to show that religious language is meaningful insofar as one plays the language game.

Again, the paragraph has a main point (implying an essay plan exists at least in the mind of the writer and very likely sketched on paper) which functions as a mini-essay in itself, with a conclusion, given by the word 'therefore' in the final sentence. It's not a waste of time to spend five minutes in the exam planning each answer and then writing for forty minutes.

In conclusion, the view proposed by Logical Positivism, that religious language is meaningless, as it cannot be empirically verified, falls short due to the fact that its stringency precludes discourse on any subjects that aren't mathematics or science. Moreover, Flew's Principle of

Falsification is lacking in that it doesn't show religious language to be totally devoid of meaning, but rather than any meaning religious language does have is given to it by those who speak it to allow them to make sense of the world. Thus it may be argued that religious language does have meaning, but that such meaning is not objective, but subjective: it is imputed by those who speak it. Wittgenstein's thought confirms this notion, demonstrating that meaning is generated by those who play a certain game and is not inherent in the game itself.

Excellent, strong thesis amply justified with an excellent range of scholarly views (scholars are also mentioned with the examples the scholars such as Hare employ - but we don't necessarily have to name scholars as long as the range of scholarly views is discussed. Here we have Hare, Wittgenstein, Ayer and Flew - plenty to consider in forty minutes). This candidate's very clear and coherent style is worth copying - it is very obvious what the answer to this particular question is and hardly a word is wasted on irrelevance (the opening sentence being perhaps the only unnecessary statement).

AO1 Level 6 (16 marks)

AO2 Level 6 (24 marks)

Overall: 40 marks Grade A*

Exercise: Rewrite the opening paragraph of this essay to include a thesis statement that sums up in one sentence the line of reasoning which the essay seeks to justify.

Ethics H573/2

Assess the view that natural law is of no help with regard to the issue of euthanasia. (40/40 A* OCR, June 2018)

Here is an answer written in the actual June 2018 exam that secured full marks. I have added comments to demonstrate what is good and not so good about this answer. You don't have to write a perfect answer to gain full marks.

Natural Law is a religious ethical theory that puts reason at the centre of moral thought and decisions. Euthanasia is a modern practice where a person/persons can be killed on their own terms, whether passively (switching of a life machine) or actively (lethal injection). In terms of the practices of euthanasia and whether it should be accepted, natural law is of no help and instead situation ethics should be adopted to the issue of euthanasia.

There are a number of good things about this opening paragraph: it has a clear thesis – situation ethics is to be preferred, although the candidate might have briefly hinted as to why. The opening emphasises reason, a point many candidates miss. And there is a clear definition of two types of euthanasia, with good issue of brackets for economy. I am not sure that euthanasia itself is an issue – there are issues involved in the moral debate such as slippery slope arguments or sanctity of life arguments. These might also have been hinted at rather than taking a broad approach.

Euthanasia is being widely adopted in modern western cultures as secularism is becoming more popular. There is more emphasis being placed on the quality of life rather than sanctity of life. Natural Law theory places special emphasis on the sanctity of life arguing that only God should have the power to take away a life.

Natural Law is an ancient theory deriving from the Greeks and particularly Aristotle.

Aquinas took Aristotle and attempted to reconcile his theory of ethics with Christianity. So what the candidate is talking about here is Aquinas' version of natural law which has been a dominant moral theory in the west, as it informs the moral theology of the Catholic Church.

There are some irrelevant assertions here such as "natural law is an ancient theory deriving from the Greeks". Much better to turn this into an analytical idea, such as 'natural law derives from a Greek teleological worldview adopted by Aristotle".

Natural Law is focused on the primary precepts and upholding its main components; worship God, live in an ordered society, reproduce, to learn and to defend the innocent. Euthanasia goes against possibly three of these primary precepts, and is therefore forbidden under natural law. The secondary precepts would argue that euthanasia is wrong as it goes against the precepts of defending the innocent. Killing someone voluntarily or non-voluntarily and worshipping God as only God should be able to take life away. In a period where quality of life is emphasised, natural law is incompatible with modern culture. Natural Law upholds the sanctity of life and any practice taking away life is wrong – in a society which allows this natural law is outdated. Aquinas lived when the church dominated society and culture and now the church and state are separate, showing now natural law should be adapted.

Aquinas finally gets a mention. The word 'adapted' is interesting as secondary precepts are meant to be adaptable, so Aquinas argues. Secondary precepts are 'proximate conclusions of reason'. The candidate hasn't really explored the tantalising hint in the first paragraph that natural law is a theory of human reason. I like the mention of three precepts here: for example, candidates often miss the implications that might exist for an ordered society if euthanasia was adopted (rise in court cases for example as relatives argue about whether passive euthanasia should be applied!).

Natural law also prohibits euthanasia on the grounds of real and apparent goods. Killing someone passively is an apparent good because it does not achieve long-term gratification as the person would be dead. However this view can be criticised as a person's suffering would be cut short so best for the long-term – there is no more suffering. Many agree with natural law also by saying that euthanasia sets a dangerous precedent and makes a possibility of a 'slippery slope' when killing becomes natural. This is against human nature.

Another weakness of natural law is that it contradicts itself. Although the primary precepts prohibit euthanasia as it actively kills a person, the doctrine of double effect allows it. If a doctor keeps prescribing a patient more medicine, which eventually leads to an overdose, this not the doctor's fault and is permissible through the doctrine of double effect. This is a weakness as it seems to contradict earlier teachings from Aquinas. However it could also be seen as a strength of natural law. The doctrine of double effect is better developed by the catholic church in response to situation ethics; it allows euthanasia to a certain degree as well as upholding religious aspects - many see this as favourable and may provide a way to treat the issue of euthanasia.

Natural law is of no use to euthanasia and so situation ethics should be adopted. Joseph Fletcher was the founder of situation ethics and was at one point president of the euthanasia society in the USA. Situation ethics allows the practice of euthanasia as it focuses on the quality of life more. Firstly, Fletcher's view of agape is much stronger as it accounts for the most loving thing to do. In certain situations, the most loving thing is to switch off the life support machine so that a person's suffering is ended. The most loving thing to do allows the families of patients to say goodbye and allows for patients to assess future possible situations themselves through living wills. Situation ethics follows the propositions of pragmatism, personalism, positivism and relativism. Each one important to the issue of euthanasia. Pragmatism allows a practical approach to euthanasia and where practicality of a situation is focused on. Personalism puts people above laws so full agape can be achieved. Although a partly legalistic theory situation ethics is also antinomian where people should be making their own decisions above the law. Positivism allows the practice of euthanasia because in most cases a positive effect is being produced. Relativism is most important because it allows the situation to be weighed on a case by case basis (natural law is unable to do this as it is absolute). These propositions provide more clarification on euthanasia and allow the issue of euthanasia to be clarified.

Natural law is not absolute in terms of its secondary precepts. To imply this simply shows that the candidate misunderstands this element of Aquinas' argument. The name Fletcher gives to his four principles is 'working principles' not 'propositions'. Notice that this paragraph is too long - proper paragraphing adds to a sense of coherence in an argument. Coherence is mentioned as an AO2 criterion of assessment.

Another supporting factor for euthanasia is the six principles which seek to fulfil agape. For example, the third principle that justice is equated to love upholds the value of love distributed. The other fundamental principles also seem to clarify how love is best served and how agape is applied in different situations. In the real case of Simon's choice, a man was diagnosed with motor neurone disease and in months ahead lost control of his bodily functions and was dependent on support. Simon made the choice to go to Switzerland to die. Natural law would not have permitted this as it breaks the precept of the sanctity of life however situation ethics would allow Simon's choice to die based on his quality of life. The shows the more practical and reasonable approach of situation ethics is more useful.

Good use of an illustrative example here.

However, situation ethics can be criticised. By describing it as relativism, euthanasia is judged on a case by case basis, which can lead to dangerous precedents. If someone is allowed to be euthanased because they are blind, it could influence other people. With sensory issues to seek euthanasia. Even if they have a decent quality of life. Euthanasia can thereby lead to a slippery slope, where euthanasia becomes too common. This raises the question of where to draw the line with euthanasia, and situation ethics provides no guidance on this. Also doctors swear by the Hippocratic Oath, to uphold the life of the patient. Situation ethics dismisses this – instead going against the doctor's primary role. A judgement is made about the future: in some cases a patient may get better. Overall however, these weaknesses don't create a strong enough basis for dismissing situation ethics.

The 'case by case basis' is actually what Fletcher means by pragmatism. Relativism means every decision is made relative to the one norm of agape, which Fletcher describes as 'principled relativism'.

On balance, therefore natural law is of no help in regard to the issue of euthanasia and instead situation ethics should be adopted. Situation ethics is stronger as it takes a teleological approach seeking to uphold the quality of life – this secures someone's autonomy and secular views which are being adopted by western societies – such as Switzerland. Natural law is also absolute and deontological, upholding the sanctity of life which seems outdated. The precepts are also incomplete with modern society Fletcher's four working principles are much more practical and relevant. Overall therefore natural law is of no help with regard to the issue of euthanasia and instead situation ethics should be adopted.

What is excellent about this essay (and often not achieved by candidates) is the precise focus on the question set. The very clear thesis is referred to again and again, elaborated and clarified. The justification for the case is complete. You can reconstruct the question from the answer itself. However, the answer is rather long and a bit repetitive. If you can develop your own slightly tighter style, it allows you to add even more excellent analysis. One glaring omission in this answer is the failure to develop and discuss the idea that natural law is a theory of human reason, which is mentioned in the opening paragraph. There are two concepts Aquinas introduces to confirm this: synderesis (the intuitive knowledge of first principles – the primary precepts) and phronesis (the practical wisdom we develop to judge secondary precepts rightly and make nuanced judgements about the application of double effect). Being critical, I also feel there are a number of misunderstandings here – about real and apparent goods, for example and the persistent claim that natural law is absolute and contains hard rules like Kantian ethics. Aquinas never argues for a hard form of deontology. Human beings are designed by God to use our reason to face hard choices and take responsibility for them.

My conclusion: to gain full marks you don't have to have knowledge that's 100% accurate, but you do need a strong argument, a clear thesis and a comprehensive analysis and evaluation that justifies your thesis. Candidates are often preparing for this exam in the wrong way – just by learning material rather than practising their analytical writing skills.

AO1 Level 6 (16 marks)

AO2 Level 6 (24 marks)

Overall 40/40 Grade A*

Exercise: Write an opening paragraph to this same question which takes a contrary view to the above candidate - namely that natural law is useful when assessing the issue of euthanasia.

'Kant's moral theory works'. Assess this view. (38/40 Grade A*)

Testing this suggestion requires clarification on what we mean by 'works'. Does this mean 'works' in the sense that it provides a coherent theory on moral action (i.e. that it makes sense as a theory) or does this mean that it 'works' in the sense that it is practically applicable to moral human questions? The two are of course related but do not necessarily follow. I will examine both aspects but concentrate my focus on the second interpretation of 'works'.

Outstanding opening paragraph, where it's clear the candidate has read the question carefully and intends to 'go for it'! There is also a twist in the thesis produced to answer the question which shows A* quality.

Kant's major assumption is in his solution to the problem of from where the idea of goodness is derived. He suggests that there are objective truths and that these can be derived through pure practical reason to generate a moral principle (which will be absolute and universal). Kant acknowledged that we have both heteronomous instincts, though we are capable of acting autonomously but fails to establish that we are perfectly rational agents, or that, even if this were so, why we <u>should</u> behave in a perfectly rational way.

I have put in a paragraph break here. Try to make one clear point per paragraph otherwise it reads like a 'stream of consciousness'.

Kant's solution to why we should act in this way is the Summum Bonum – a state of affairs where goodness and happiness are achieved but for Kant only in the afterlife could or would this be fully realised. So for Kant, we may have to sacrifice happiness in the short term (for example we might choose to tell a truth that is hurtful – as an extreme case the murderer at the door problem) but we can do so in the knowledge that there is a purpose to this moral behaviour. But, Kant needs to acknowledge the existence of an eternal life as a necessary feature of a fair universe to explain how his theory is just (a fair distribution of happiness) therefore Kant said that there were three postulates – freedom, immorality and God – which he believed were necessary conditions for morality. 'The highest good is practically possible only on the supposition of the immortality of the soul…God'. Therefore, despite all Kant's focus on rationality, he must explain the idea of goodness, and the question of why I should be moral, by making a metaphysical assumption and on this basis, Kant's moral theory does not 'work' as coherent theory, unless I believe.

Excellent point. There is indeed something strange about constructing a theory around human autonomy and then requiring a metaphysical assumption to create a desirable end. It's good to mention the summum bonum, even if the specification omits to mention it.

Does Kant create a moral theory that works in practical application? For Kant only acting through Duty and the Goodwill can an action be moral. We can reach an understanding of these terms through our application of reason but Kant makes an important distinction to help clarify a moral action. We must not act according to a Hypothetical Imperative (a command in a conditional form) but a Categorical Imperative – the law of autonomous will derived from Duty. The three tests of the Categorical Imperative do however have problems. The most well known is the Principle of Universal Law, which in practical terms means that I should ask 'am I willing that this action should always be followed by everyone in every situation'.

I have again had to insert a paragraph break here.

There have been two criticisms made of this. First, Rachels suggests that one can simply universalise a decision to such a specific extent that it would be easily universalizable – I might lie to save a friend when there is a deranged lunatic at the door and in any cases where there is a deranged lunatic at the door I would wish others to act in the same way. 'All that is required by Kant's basic idea is that when we violate a rule, we do so for a reason that we would be willing for anyone to accept, were they in our position' (Rachels). However, Kant is very clear on this point in his Groundwork that that it would be wrong to 'over-particularize the maxim', making the rule so specific it would be universalized with ease. Despite being wrong in his interpretation of Kant the fact that Rachels is wrong and Kant insists on not 'over-particularizing' makes Kant's moral theory unworkable in a practical sense.

I have inserted yet another paragraph break here. The paragraph above would be better if you'd argued it the other way round – begun with Kantian rigidity and the crazy axe murderer and then said "However, Rachels argues that…"

It is also vulnerable to the objections of rigidity and cold-heartedness (Arrington) and in the words of Bernard Williams 'atomistic' approach to ethics that causes an individual to make a moral choice that seems to reject a loving human nature (the murderer at the door problem, or decisions that might be made around other ethical problems such as euthanasia or abortion for example). Modern philosophers have to some degree attempted to revisit Kant's idea with the caveat of allowing a more 'particularising' approach (RM Hare and Bernard Williams) and while sacrificing the strict deontology do make the idea more workable.

I don't think the candidate has made the cold-hearted point very clear – which is then linked to the idea of love. Here we see how Kant backs himself into a corner – if we just use our rationality and ignore our emotion, what happens to motives such as love, or even empathy?

Kant's second test of the Categorical Imperative, The Principle of Ends is a considerable strength of his moral theory. It suggests that we should universalise our common humanity, implying equality, that every human agent has absolute worth: 'Act so that you treat humanity, both in your own person and in the person of every other human being, never merely as a means, but always at the same time as an end'. Problems with this formula have been suggested in that it seems to tie rationality to humanity and as such he comes up for criticism in the same manner that Peter Singer faces in modern times about the rights of the mentally disabled for instance. Kant however, rejected these criticisms. The bigger problem for Kant is that he considered that the tests for the Categorical Imperative were not isolated from each other and as such a moral decision had to satisfy all three tests, which again raises the issues previously stated with the first formula.

Yes, good to quote the Kantian formula, and to quote it correctly! It works, though, as underpinning a theory of universal human rights. Not sure the Singer point is made very clear.

I do not believe that Kant's moral theory works in the sense of being a coherent moral theory or being practically applicable. Kant's Enlightenment insistence on finding a rational and deontological approach means that it is 'like a man who starves for want of a dinner jacket' (Simon Blackburn). It forces actions that take no account of the emotional and humanitarian outcomes or an insistence that there will be a greater good eventually (Summum Bonum). However, Kant's legacy does have importance with respect to a universal dignity, in the Declaration of Human Rights and International Law. Kant's moral theory does not work but aspects of his theory are vital for modern philosophy to reject emotivism and relativism in the twenty-first century.

An excellent answer. This is a bold answer with a strong thesis, and so much better for it – courage pays off in exams. The candidate constructs a very clear and coherent thesis. The thesis is consistently related to the question set. The candidate uses quotes and bounce his/her own thoughts off these quotes. Key terms such as summum bonum are also used rather well. Note that the phrase summum bonum is not contained in the specification, but it is a good idea nonetheless to use a philosopher's own terms, carefully considered and defined. I would, however, have liked a slightly clearer explanation of how the idea of universalisability works – maybe use an example, but nonetheless the candidate criticises this key idea very effectively. Kant wants us to take an imaginative leap out of a situation in the name of consistency. It is also good that the candidate doesn't try to explain three formulations of the categorical imperative (many less confident students do, and it is not necessary; indeed it can make the essay read as a processional list. I would argue that you only really need two out of three formulae – even though the specification mentions three).

It is the process of Kantian reasoning that needs to be made explicit, not a description of various formula, and here this essay scores highly.

AO1 Level 6 (15 marks)

AO2 Level 6 (23 marks)

Overall 38/40 A*

Exercise: Take this question "Kantian ethics is the hard-nosed ethic of duty'. Discuss

- *Practise a five paragraph plan..*

- *Insert analytical words or phrases to start different paragraphs (however, moreover, furthermore, on the other hand etc). A list is at the back of this book.*

- *Essay planning – one main point per paragraph, with a contrast, a quote or an evaluative twist. A level answers should weave together analysis and evaluation – which means you bring out what we call AO1 and AO2 criteria.*

Situation Ethics is unworkable in practice. Discuss (40/40, Grade A*)

The workability of situation ethics could mean the ease of identifying a norm to use, the ease of application of the norm, or the realism of the theory itself. It could be argued situation ethics fails on all three counts, as the author William Barclay suggests in his book Ethics in a Permissive Society.

The candidate doesn't make the mistake of trying to say everything in summary in the opening paragraph. Instead, there is concise discussion of 'unworkable'. Always raise issue around key words in the title.

Situation ethics claims a simple, easy to define norm, that of agape love. Agape love means sacrificial love for friend or stranger. In reality it is a difficult norm to define because it implies impartiality, strict neutrality in the observe and what utilitarian Peter Singer calls the universal viewpoint. If my interests spread out from me like ripples of a pond, I naturally place my immediate family first, my friends second, and my acquaintances, third. People who are strangers lie many circles beyond immediate circles of interest. By implying impartiality, the norm of agape love is therefore both unrealistic and almost impossible to apply in practice. Which stranger do I include, and how many?

Good. Many candidates take an uncritical view of situation ethics which is arguably a difficult, challenging and demanding normative theory. Good use of another scholar - preference utilitarian Singer is famous for his 'universal viewpoint' - which is an idea requiring quite heroic sacrifice.

The parable of the Good Samaritan illustrates just how demanding love is. The battered man is rescued by the Samaritan who uses his donkey as transport, where priest and levite has passed by without stopping. The Samaritan even pays the bill and offers to repay any debts the innkeeper should encounter in caring for the injured man. This type of love, although incarnated by Jesus Christ, is impossible for most of us as well as being unreasonable. No wonder Fletcher posits Positivism as one of his working principles. Positivism means we are supposed to accept situation ethics by faith, on trust. Even if we are able to do this heroic acceptance, it is nonetheless just too demanding a norm.

Excellent use of an example to show how agape works and synoptically linking this to the Moral Principles part of the Christian Thought paper. You get AO2 credit for making synoptic links.

Barclay indicates a more serious problem. Situation ethics is situated between legalism and antinomianism, between adherence to the law and an anarchic disdain for law. Yet it is unclear in Fletcher's theory exactly what role law plays. Comparing, for example, situation ethics with Mill's rule utilitarianism, we can see that Mill argues we should generally follow rules until our own wisdom suggest that there is a moral conflict where something has to go. For example, in euthanasia cases you cannot always preserve life and also alleviate pain: the opiod can kill you as a physician induced act of mercy.

Good critical AO2 comment here. Good use of an additional scholar - candidates should be familiar with William Barclay who is listed in the suggested reading on the specification.

Therefore, the place of law is important in society at least in preserving a barrier between simple choice (to kill a patient) and a moral dilemma (when you can't have both moral 'goods'). Barclay points out that society needs rules to provide a coherence to its public morality, and also to show the wisdom of previous generations. Rules pass on that wisdom and provide a basis for moral education. Rules of course don't have to be absolute as the Bible itself shows: 'do not kill' cannot include killing in times of war as the Bible also permits the military campaigns of Joshua. But by failing to recognise the role of rules, Fletcher adds to the problems of situation ethics – it becomes unworkable because it places too much responsibility on individual judgement.

Excellent paragraph again showing a blend of knowledge (of absolutes and what they might mean) and a strong AO2 line of reasoning.

Finally two further working principles add to the problem with the ethics. Personalism implies we take the individual needs seriously and place them as a priority. But individuals do not exist in a vacuum. When a teenager chooses to take drugs, it affects everyone: family, school, friends and society which pays the bill for treatment. Situation ethics is in danger of becoming a narrow, almost selfish ethic (ironically as agape is selfless love). And pragmatism implies we proceed case by case. Apparently we abandon rules, the social context and the idea of society itself in simply concentrating on the case in front of us. This too is, I argue, impossible in practice.

Good reference back to the four working principles. The candidate has not mentioned the fourth one, relativism, which basically means that you 'relativise the absolute' the absolute being the unchangeable norm of agape. It is made relative always to the circumstances argues Fletcher. Paradoxically he calls his theory 'principled relativism'.

In conclusion: in concentrating just on the supreme norm of agape and its too demanding nature, by analysing the four working principles and assessing their workability we can see that situation ethics is superficially attractive (all we need is love) but practically unworkable. Moreover as Barclay suggests, we cannot wisely do without rules, nor underplay their value in building a workable ethic.

AO1 Level 6 (16 marks)

AO2 Level 6 (24 marks)

This essay is shorter than many of the A* answers in the section on this book. But it illustrates something the examiner reminds us about in the June 2018 report: it is not length that matters. The essay shouldn't be a knowledge display. Notice how the candidate never mentions any background to Joseph Fletcher, the decade he wrote in (the 1960s) or anything extraneous at all. It is a lean, tightly argued essay.

Exercise: write an opening paragraph on the same title above taking the opposite viewpoint (ie that situation ethics is workable).

'Good is meaningful'. Discuss (33/40 Grade A, OCR June 2018)

Many scholars such as AJ Ayer would suggest that 'good' is meaningless, because it cannot be verified analytically or synthetically, placing it in the category of subjective opinion, based solely on emotion. Although I would agree with Ayer that moral statements are just expressions of emotion, I would be Inclined to suggest that these statements still have meaning, as they are part of our daily lives, through law and basic human rights.

A Good, clear introduction laying out the parameters of the question in terms of analytic and synthetic truth. Strictly speaking, you don't verify analytic statements as they are true by definition and do not require empirical observations to confirm them. The truth value is internal to the meaning itself. The phrase 'based solely on emotion' is also not quite right: moral statements express emotion, but that doesn't necessarily they are just based on emotion. This is meta-ethics – about the meaning of the language, not normative ethics which explores the basis for such a judgement. Ayer's is a meta-ethical claim.

Bradley in his book "Ethical Naturalism' would suggest that good is an absolute, observable fact of the world, which has direct relevance to our position and role in society. This would imply that good has a resolute meaning as it influences how we should behave, given our place in the world. Many thinkers would criticise this viewpoint, such as Kai Neilson who would correctly note that society is ever-changing, and 'good' varies within different cultures, which would adequately explain our changing attitudes to homosexuality, pre-marital sex and race and diversity.

'Absolute' is rather an ambiguous term in ethics. It can mean universal – applying to the whole of humanity, objective, meaning measurable in some way, or non-consequentialist. When Bradley speaks of 'something beyond' I think he means we can point to something observable or at least part of our common experience (such as utilitarian pleasure and pain). It would be good to mention the naturalistic fallacy here, because the debate in meta-ethics is whether we can really point meaningfully to this 'something beyond'. This student could really do with referring back to the question and bring out, and discuss, the idea of what 'meaningfulness' might imply to different authors. Generally it's always a good idea to keep retranslating and reworking the question specifically in each paragraph.

This would suggest that other naturalists, such as Philippa Foot, are incorrect to say that good has a fixed meaning, even if it is culturally observable as to what societies mean by 'good'. Foot uses the insightful example from Memoirs of a Revolutionist to try and illustrate how 'good' is something fixed and intrinsically meaningful. The example states how a geographer , observing a tribe of indigenous people, upholds his promise not to photograph them even when he is presented with the opportunity of doing so without their knowledge of it, whilst they are asleep. This, Foot would argue, illustrates how 'good' is a fixed duty and not relative to the people concerned, but concrete.

Again, the candidate needs to refer back to the question and make the idea of meaningfulness explicit. What is the 'something beyond' which Foot is pointing to? Isn't it Aristotelean eudaimonia, a state where our potential is fulfilled by observing those rules which objectively build a better world for us – a world where our potential is more likely to be fulfilled/ Honesty of character and truthfulness build an objectively (measurably) better world.

Perhaps Kant's maxim of 'universalisation' could suggest a reason for this apparently 'fixed' sense of duty from the geographer. This could be suggested as perhaps the geographer would not want this action to be universalised, and if he was in the situation would not want someone to take a picture of him, hence suggesting that self-preference and compassion for others decides goodness; it is not fixed but relative and therefore has meaning only in a subjective sense.

It's not entirely clear how Kant relates to the point about absolute versus relative morality, as of course Kant argued that feelings of compassion were irrelevant for morality and only duty for duty's sake counted as a motive.

Mackie makes an interesting addition to this debate in his book 'Does Morality Rest on a Mistake' as he suggests that we know what good is and it has meaning; but that this 'meaning' is completely made up by society and tradition. He gives the example of the rules in a game of chess, which are only valid due to the being created and accepted by those who play, and have no meaning to someone who did not know how to play the game. This suggestion that good has meaning which is actually human created would provide a much more satisfactory explanation of that of an intuitionist such as GE Moore, who in Principia Ethica would argue that "when I am asked 'what is good?' my answer is 'good is just good' and that is the end of the matter".

This suggests that good is indefinable but still has intrinsic meaning as just as we recognise the colour yellow, we intrinsically recognise good, suggesting that it has significant meaning, even if some would argue this definition of it lacks clarity.

Yes, this is the key point.

In conclusion, ethical naturalists and intuitionists alike, although disagreeing how to define good, or whether it can indeed be defined, would both suggest that good does indeed have meaning. Personally I would suggest that Kai Neilson's principle of cultural relativism sheds the most light on this issue, although he states that good is essentially made up it still has different meaning in different cultures, even although it cannot be empirically or analytically proven.

A very clear piece of writing which takes a particular line on the question and sustains that line successfully, embracing a wide range of scholarly views. I would have liked to see the Ayer/Hume point developed a bit more at the start, but notwithstanding this, it is a good A grade answer beautifully written.

AO1 Level 5 (13 marks)

A very good attempt to address the question demonstrating knowledge and understanding. Very good selection of relevant material, technical terms mostly accurate. a very good range of scholarly views, academic approaches, and/or sources of wisdom and authority are used to demonstrate knowledge and understanding

AO2 Level 5 (20 marks)

A very good demonstration of analysis and evaluation in response to the question. successful and clear analysis, evaluation and argument. Views very well stated, coherently developed and justified. There is a well–developed and sustained line of reasoning which is coherent, relevant and logically structured.

Overall: 33/40 83% A

Exercise: do some original research on the issue of naturalism and the naturalistic fallacy and write a paragraph on this subject - 'the naturalistic fallacy is itself a fallacy'. This is a chance to show originality and insight (two things the examiner complained were lacking in the June 2018 answers).

'Doing the right thing by stakeholders also benefits shareholders.' Discuss. (23/40 Grade C)

Robert W. Lane, the Chairman and CEO of Deere & Company has stated that: "If you don't have honesty and integrity, you won't be able to develop effective relationships with any of your stakeholders." This is the basis of an ethical approach to relationships within business.

In your opening paragraph it's wiser to define the key terms (eg stakeholders) and then state your thesis – which is a one line summary of your position.

Stakeholders are extremely important, as they form the basis of success and failure of any business. They are individuals or groups that have interests, rights, or ownership in an organisation and its activities. Customers, suppliers, employees, and shareholders are examples of primary stakeholder groups. Each group has its own particular interests in how an organisation performs or interacts with them, and they can benefit from a company's success or be harmed by its mistakes. As stock(share)holders are also primary stakeholders, doing the right thing by stakeholders will usually benefit the shareholders too – they are part of the same group.

Shareholders are legal owners of the company and gain in two ways: by increased share values and by the payment of annual dividends. The problem is: the interests of different stakeholders may be in conflict eg employees want higher wages and shareholders want higher share values.

However, secondary stakeholders are also important because they can take action that can damage or assist the organisation. Secondary stakeholders include governments (especially through regulatory agencies), unions, nongovernmental organisations (NGOs), political action groups, and even the media and the environment. It is in this area that there may be conflict between what is good for stakeholders and what is good for shareholders.

In order to serve their stakeholders (including shareholders) in an ethical and social manner, more and more organisations are adapting the model of corporate social responsibility, the objective of which is to be socially responsible, while at the same time meeting or exceeding the expectations of all its stakeholders. One aspect of social responsibility is economic responsibility. Businesses are, above all, the basic economic unit of society, with a responsibility to produce goods and services and to maximise profit for their owners and shareholders.

The candidate needs to discuss the question in front of you rather than just describe different forms of stakeholder.

Treating economic responsibility as the most important responsibility of a business is called a profit-maximizing view, a term coined by Nobel economist Milton Friedman. This view states that a company should be operated on a profit-oriented basis, with its sole mission to increase its profits. This approach would certainly seem to benefit primary stakeholders, including shareholders. However, a problem can occur when businesses struggle to balance ethical responsibility to provide shareholders with their rightful returns and corporate social responsibility

– if they seem more concerned with profit they can be perceived as greedy and avaricious.

Yes but see the comment I made earlier about conflicting interests of different stakeholders.

There are certainly companies out to milk society in the name of greed, but it is important to note that companies do have a very real <u>financial</u> responsibility to shareholders and thus must include economic responsibility as one of their top priorities. If a company focuses too hard on corporate social responsibility and ignores shareholders in the process, this can have a detrimental effect on all concerned. Eventually shareholders will stop <u>investing</u> if they don't see a return on their investment. If people stop investing, businesses will have difficulty getting funding; if a company fails, individuals lose jobs; and if the company is large enough, local economies can be severely impacted. All organisations, even non-profitable ones, need to generate revenue in order to remain operational. Any organisation that hopes to be in business for the long term has to consider their shareholders.

This is a much more interesting paragraph – again relate it back to the question. It begins however with a gross generalisation which needs to be substantiated - about companies setting out to milk society.

While this will definitely do the right thing by the shareholders, secondary stakeholders such as the environment may lose out. Therefore, many business ethicists no longer consider the purely profit-maximising view as morally appropriate. Treating economic gain as the only responsibility can lead companies into trouble. A company which behaves in ways inconsistent with the values of its customers, employees, or community will find itself being corrected in any number of ways, ranging from losing individual customers or employees, to formal boycotts, or even legal action. Trying to increase profitability by ignoring ethical concerns will eventually wind up costing the company money, negating any short-term benefit to stakeholders and shareholders. This is particularly true today, when information can spread rapidly through the Internet, and both customers and employees have an enormous range of options. Therefore treating the stakeholders well will have a knock-on effect on the shareholders. Sometimes, behaving ethically may require a company to take a longer view, and sacrifice some profit today for the sake of building goodwill and a strong reputation. Recent examples of this include Nike, Gap and Primark changing their policies regarding child labour and Monsanto's over GM food.

Yes, this paragraph relates much more strongly to the question. How you relate to the question is part of the criteria of assessment included in the word 'engagement' discussed in the opening chapter.

On the other hand, an organisation which is seen to be actively taking responsibility for the environment (e.g. the Body Shop) or fair treatment of workers (e.g. Fairtrade), often maintains a positive reputation which attracts more consumers and converts to profits which benefits everyone; however a business that is struggling sometimes has to make difficult choices and as a priority does have to consider its shareholders first. In this situation, what will prove most beneficial to the stakeholders may not be the same as for shareholders.

Marc Epstein and Karen Schneitz have argued that corporate responsibility plays an important part in increasing and preserving shareholder value. Scholars have long debated whether firms should spend money on improving social and environmental performance. Supporters say that it is ethically important for businesses to play a responsible role in society. In contrast, opponents argue that taking care of broad stakeholder groups, other than firms' immediate owners and employees, is the role of government--not business. However, if a business is perceived by the consumer and wider public to be shirking its moral responsibilities towards either primary or secondary stakeholders, experience has proved that they will withdraw their support and custom. This has detrimental effects on both stakeholders and shareholders. Therefore, the statement that 'doing the right thing by stakeholders also benefits the stock(share)holders' does seem to be correct.

Rather generalised. Milton Friedman is one economist who argues that it is the role of Government to set the moral parameters. An example might ground this paragraph - and the example might actually disprove the main point as very few businesses in reality find their customers deserting them (research BP and the Gulf of Mexico oil spill or VW and the diesel emissions scandal).

The candidate makes some interesting points in this essay and the overall feel of the essay is strengthened by the conclusion. However, the weakness of the essay lies in the failure to really unpack, discuss, and consider carefully the issues underlying the question. Think of the many companies that are accused of mistreating their workers – recently Amazon (underpaying, overworking), Pret a Manger (underpaying in the USA), zero hour contracts (widespread in UK) etc. Their share price has been unaffected by these allegations. So I suggest that paying attention to stakeholders only applies (arguably) if ethical business practices are a strong part of your brand image.

Try to write an opening paragraph that maps out the territory and then presents a thesis statement in response to the question set.

AO1 Level 3 (7 marks)

A satisfactory demonstration of knowledge and understanding with of mostly relevant material. Some accurate knowledge demonstrating understanding through material used but may be lacking in breadth. Sources and academic approaches are used to demonstrate knowledge and understanding with only partial success

AO2 Level 4 (16 marks)

A good demonstration of analysis and evaluation in response to the question. Generally successful analysis, evaluation and argument. Views well stated, with some development and justification. Answers the question set well. There is a well–developed line of reasoning which is clear, relevant and logically structured.

Assessment of Extended Response: There is a well–developed line of reasoning which is clear, relevant and logically structured

Exercise: Write your own answer to the essay question above, aiming to gain at least level 5 - and then swap essays with a friend and mark each other's. Only write for 40 minutes (but use a plan if necessary).

Evaluate Aquinas' theological approach to conscience. (26/40 Grade B, OCR June 2018)

Aquinas, writing in the thirteenth century with a theological approach, is, for its time, the closest thing to a psychological approach to conscience thought of. It shares many aspects with Freud's more modern analysis of the conscience, such as the idea of guilt and desire. Consequently it can be called a logical, structured approach to conscience as although it is reliant on the existence of God, it gives us good insights into the human mind.

This opening paragraph illustrates quote well a tactical mistake – introducing a very interesting but tangential point about Freud without first establishing what is meant by a 'theological approach to conscience". Indeed as you read on through the essay you will notice how the 'theological approach' itself becomes an assumed thing without being properly and fully brought out into the open. The point about Freud is fascinating and potentially very good, but should have been woven into the analysis. The first paragraph should be reserved for attacking (unpacking) the question and then presenting a brief outline of your approach and your controlling thesis.

Aquinas in Summa Theologica would argue that reason distinguishes us from animals, as we are made 'in the image of God' or 'imago dei', and that we must use reason or 'ratio' to distinguish the best moral decisions to make. He believes that humans have a natural orientation towards the good (synderesis) that guides us and helps our ratio to make right choices as it is infallible. Many, such as Vardy and Grosch would argue against this notion of synderesis, as human nature is essentially corruptible, and not naturally orientated towards the good. This could be supported by Aristotle's 'doctrine of habituation' which interestingly suggests that people learn what good and bad is when they are children, and have to be 'habituated' to the societal norms and expectations.

This is a very good paragraph but again needs to be openly related to the question and the word 'theological'. Paul could also be used to illustrate the imago dei point as Paul says in Romans 2 that even the Gentiles have the 'law written on their hearts'. I am not sure the explanation for ratio is quite right here. It is ratio which is inherent in the divine blueprint for the world – God's reasoning in terms of telos, proper purpose. We develop phronesis or practical wisdom to guide us in moral decision-making – and so we have two moral and theological developments of general ratio, synderesis and phronesis. Neither phronesis nor synderesis has to be inherently theological or given by God, however. Synderesis is very close to Dawkins' altruistic gene, and he definitely is not arguing theologically.

Consequently it would seem likely that Aquinas' theological notion of 'synderesis' is accurate but that perhaps it is not God-given, but instead learnt from parents and society, which would be supported by Freud in 'An Outline to Psychoanalysis' also.

'Theological' here means 'God-given' and "God-designed'. Good evaluative point to say that the inherent moral sense could come from somewhere else – society and parents (Freud) or evolution (Dawkins).

Furthermore, Aquinas' notion of 'sensuality', which he believes to be the part of us that tempts us away from God, and was responsible for the Fall in the Garden of Eden, has merit in line with Freud's notion of the Id as both seeking pleasures outside of what is expected (whether by God for Aquinas, or by society for Freud). Freud believed that these desires were sexual, repressed and driven by the libido, which could link to the fact that in the post-lapsarian state many scholars such as Augustine believe that sex is tainted by sin and lust, as before the Fall it was a duty and not a pleasure, and after is associated with concupiscence. This suggests that Aquinas' notion of 'sensuality' as a temptation away from correctly informed decisions using reason is accurate, as there is certainly stigma around sex and 'original sin' for many Catholic thinkers.

I'm not entirely sure how this paragraph relates to the actual question set and again it reveals a tactical mistake by the candidate – to present a clearer question-related thesis rather than divert slightly into these very interesting, but ultimately perhaps not mainstream points. The paragraph could have been made more clearly relevant by saying something like "synderesis assumes a general orientation by our very natures towards the moral good, defined as morally good ends. However, there are certain natural tendencies within humankind which beg the question, what exactly is the moral good? Sex is one such area, where for example, the theological approach has been interpreted as forbidding sex outside marriage and labelling desire as itself inherently evil – a product of concupiscence and the Fall of human kind. It is hard to reconcile synderesis as interpreted by Aquinas and the modern view of sexual feelings or indeed, homosexual orientation'.

The fact that Aquinas recognises that this sense of 'ratio' is fallible, as it is based on knowledge (*nb the candidate doesn't make this point clear, unfortunately*) also adds to the strength of his argument about conscience. He recognises that through 'vincible' or 'invincible' error our judgements can be faulty, either because we did not take time to inform ourselves of all the facts, or because we could not possibly have known all the facts of the situation, and therefore are not at fault. This perceptively takes into account the faltering nature of human conscience, as humans are always going to make moral mistakes.

Fair point to introduce vincible and invincible ignorance which is Aquinas' attempt to reconcile the fact of imago dei goodness with the fact that we obviously sin and do horrible things.

In conclusion, Aquinas' theological approach to conscience has several merits, as it takes into account the desire to stray from what is right (sensuality) and also suggests that we are conditioned to 'know' what is good and what is bad. Although this might come from human punishment or reward when we are children, it still accurately describes the process at work in our mind when we are faced with a moral decision.

Good clear conclusion. Generally this candidate writes very well, with a beautifully clear style. I repeat my earlier point – there is a problem of exam tactics in the failure to continually keep the question in the forefront of the answer and address it clearly in every paragraph. I feel a clearer thesis statement would have helped in the opening paragraph stating what a theological approach means and what is in outline good and bad about Aquinas' view. Then Dawkins and Freud could have been introduced as counter-points and the candidate would have got close to full marks.

AO1 Level 4 (10 marks)

A good demonstration of knowledge and understanding. Addresses the question well. Good selection of relevant material, used appropriately on the whole. Mostly accurate knowledge which demonstrates good understanding of the material used, which should have reasonable amounts of depth or breadth. A good range of scholarly views

AO2 Level 4 (16 marks)

A good demonstration of analysis and evaluation in response to the question. Generally successful analysis, evaluation and argument. Views well stated, with some development and justification. Answers the question set well. There is a well–developed line of reasoning which is clear, relevant and logically structured.

Overall 26/40 65% Grade B

Exercise: Write a paragraph explaining why **neither** Aquinas nor Freud argue that conscience is the 'voice of God'. Use some analytical words and phrases contained in the appendix to this book.

Critically assess the view that Utilitarianism is of no use when making decisions about sexual ethics. (38/40, Grade A*)

It is not fair to say that Utilitarianism is of no use at all when making decisions about sexual ethics. It can provide a useful tool when considering such issues in many cases. However, it seems that if 'use' is taken to mean clarity of decision making in a practical sense, Natural Law would be a better alternative on, for example, contraception in providing a clear response. A theory's usefulness depends on your definition. Thus, with different definitions, Utilitarianism's use can change.

Yes. This is an excellent opening paragraph because the candidate has noticed that the idea of 'usefulness' needs some meaning imposed on it - otherwise the essay will not know what the target issue is to discuss. Suggest a couple of outline reasons after the opening sentence to move this away from being just an assertion. Note that contraception is no longer on the specification, but it still forms a good example of an important issue in sexual ethics.

One important area of sexual ethics is the issue of contraception as the intoduction of the pill changed the nature of human autonomy. A utilitarian approach may be considered of use when applying to contraception, when use is defined as fitting in to modern society. Utilitarianism considers the maximising happiness and minimising pain. It must consider the consequences of an action. It can be said that using contraception does provide the greatest happiness of the greatest number. The two people who participate (consensually) will gain pleasure from the act and the consequence of becoming pregnant is avoided. Therefore, it would seem that utilitarianism would support the use of contraception in cases where the woman does not want to become pregnant.

A good, balanced paragraph.

However a fatal flaw with utilitarianism is its difficulty in predicting consequences. Using contraception may prevent a baby being born. Is it right that the happiness of a future human is not counted? Moreover, the hedonic calculus, initiated by Jeremy Bentham, takes into account such things as the duration, intensity and certainty of the happiness. When using contraception, the prediction is that the woman and man would be happier without a child. However, this cannot be proven. When the decision is made, this might be the view of the people involved, but it may not be the same in the future. Therefore, although utilitarianism in some cases may provide useful, it cannot always be trusted due to the complexity of predicting consequences.

A good number of A02 level 6 points are being made here. Notice the use of 'moreover' and 'however' in this paragraph.

Bentham was very keen at looking at the greatest happiness for the greatest number. Thus, even an action taken by two people must consider the implications for others as well. In cases where the contraception used is the morning after pill or a similar method of contraception, opinion is more divided. By this point, the sperm may have already fertilised the egg and the contraception may take the form of a very early abortion. Utilitarianism must then decide what accounts as a person included in its formula. For a Catholic, a foetus counts as human at the moment of conception. If this view were taken, it would make it even more difficult to apply the Hedonic Calculus

Difficult to apply because - the candidate needs to explain why?.

However, Peter Singer, a preference utilitarian, would argue that sentient beings classify as persons. Thus, a foetus formed very soon after conception would not count as a person. Peter Singer would not take into account its preferences when making a decision. The preferences of others would be taken into account, and a decision would be made relatively easily. Bentham's act utilitarianism would be a lot more difficult to apply as the consequences of using contraception are just too difficult. It is not a practical, clear theory for dealing with contraception.

This weakness of utilitarianism contrasts directly with Natural Law's strength. Thomas Aquinas' Natural Law presents a clear straight forward answer to the issue of contraception. For Aquinas, one must refer to the primary precepts. Contraception goes against preferring life and thus a secondary precept would be "do not use contraception". In the Catholic Church, reproduction is a clear message to follow and is important: "Go forth and multiply". Thus, using contraception would be going against God's word. It is important to note that as well as reproduction, pleasure and unity are also important. While sex without contraception satisfies all three, sex with contraception cannot. This adds to Aquinas' belief that contraception is wrong. Although Natural Law offers a clear formulation, it does not give a conclusion that is consistent with the modern age. Nowadays, with contraception free on the NHS and a customary action to use contraception, it is difficult to see how Natural Law fits in. In this sense, utilitarianism, particularly preference, is a better method, and certainly not of no use.

Reproduction is more than a message - it's arguably a fundamental moral good. It might fit in if we could come to some agreement that social eudaimonia requires us to limit or eliminate our use of contraception - but I agree it's rather difficult to see how in an age of overpopulation.

Furthermore, utilitarianism is of a lot of use when making decisions about homosexuality. JS Mill's Rule Utilitarianism considers not only maximising happiness, but also preferring higher pleasures. Homosexuality allows the couple to be happy, a happiness that also outweighs anyone else's pain from disagreeing with homosexuality. Considering Mill, a homosexual couple means the higher pleasure of love and sharing their intellectual power is important. Therefore, it would seem that utilitarianism would support homosexuality, as it provides happiness for those involved, just as a heterosexual relationship would do. Not only does this provide a clear response, but it also agrees with the position of modern society at the moment. It is of use, therefore, in two ways.

Some ambiguity in this paragraph eg the phrase 'intellectual power'. There are both social and personal consequences which need to be distinguished here as Mill put a great emphasis on the social context of our happiness.

Contrast this with Natural Law, which would be against homosexuality due to it going against the primary precept to preserve life, and utilitarianism is a far more useful theory to make decisions about sexual ethics. With homosexuality, utilitarianism is more useful than with contraception, because the consequences are less complicated to discern, making the decision easier to make.

Natural Law theorists don't have to agree with the Roman Catholic interpretation of secondary precepts. Indeed the Catholic church has a more absolute view of secondary precepts than Aquinas ever envisaged.

Therefore, I do not think that Utilitarianism is of no use when considering sexual ethics. Utilitarianism can be of use when considering issues such as homosexuality. This is particularly because as a relativist theory, it can agree with the changing ideas of society. Moreover, it takes into account peoples preferences, increasing the importance of the individual and not just providing rules as Natural Law does. However, utilitarianism is limited in its usefulness. When it comes to decisions about issues such as contraception, consequences are immensely hard to predict. Thus Utilitarianism becomes a guessing game, reducing its reliability and thus, its usefulness. It still remains that Utilitarianism can remain of use when considering sexual ethics.

A very good essay which demonstrates a high level of analytical and evaluative technique, discusses the question fully, imposes a line on the ambiguity within the question (the meaning of 'useful') and provides a throughly clear answer. This candidate does, however, sometimes lapse into unexplained assertions - see my comments in between paragraphs, which is unfortunate in that the potential is there to gain full marks if this habit had been eliminated.

AO1 Level 6 (15 marks)

AO2 Level 6 (23 marks)

Overall 38/40 Grade A*

Exercise: Prepare a table with an outline of all the ethical theories (Natural Law, Situation Ethics, Utilitarianism and Kantian ethics) in the first column and a summary of each of their approaches in the second column. Now right a paragraph on the following question, substituting your favourite theory for X:

"X is the best approach to issues surrounding sexual ethics".

Christian Thought Paper H573/3

Assess the view that Augustine's teaching on human nature is too pessimistic. (30/40, Grade A/B)

To say that Augustine's teaching on human nature is too pessimistic implies that it offers little hope to Christians today. If this is true then perhaps the Christian hope in salvation and eternal happiness is misplaced. Scholars such as Freud for example, hold some beliefs that are similar to Augustine's and some that are not, he rejects Augustine's view that original sin from Adam and Eve is transmitted through sex, however, does not deny the importance of libido, Freud is much more optimistic. Additionally, Dawkins, for example, would support the idea that Augustine's teaching is too pessimistic, however, Niebuhr holds beliefs very similar to Augustine and is fairly pessimistic towards human nature, but not as much as Augustine. I think Augustine's teaching is 'too pessimistic', there is not really anything positive about it, however, if you appreciate the 'cure' offered by God's grace and faith then it lowers the pessimism slightly.

A promising start at signposting an argument that considers the extent to which Augustine would be pessimistic. Scholars are referred to.

Firstly, Augustine's explanation of men and women before the Fall was one of peace and harmony, Adam and Eve had a perfect friendship and the body and will was in harmony too. Their relationship is described as concordia, they were living in a state of the very best possible human relationships. However, the rebellious will caused the Fall – a disobedience. This led to disharmony and a divided will; Augustine believes the will is now incapable of controlling the natural desires of the body in the post-Lapsarian world. This rebellious will is also seen in our failure to live in society according to God's will.

Good technicality but needs developing with examples – e.g. quote from Genesis – how is their friendship shown?

I believe Augustine's teaching on human nature is too pessimistic. Firstly, because if the Fall has destroyed human free will, then there is nothing we can do to overcome original sin. This is because, this original sin is passed on through generations seminally, according to Augustine. Original sin being passed through sexual intercourse causes human selfishness, lack of free will, lack of stability and corruption in all human societies. I highly disagree with this, is an absolutely crazy and an insane concept and biologically impossible to pass on sin but only genes and sexual disorders. Sin is an ontological condition of humankind, rather than sin being something we are 'prone to', it is part of the essence of who we are. We might appear virtuous, but no one is good. However, Pelagious disagrees, although Adam set a poor example we can still try to live morally. I agree with this, because surely mistakes are part of out human nature but that does not make as a whole sinful and therefore means we need to be redeemed by God, it just means we need to learn from our mistakes and move on, no one is perfect and it is inevitable that we will do the wrong thing from time to time.

Avoid emotive language such as 'absolutely crazy and insane' as this spoils the academic feel of the analysis. Examples needed to support the points in this paragraph.

However, Augustine disagrees, he believes human efforts alone were not enough, we need God's grace and Christ's presence. Again I disagree and believe this is a very pessimistic view of human nature, because the Christian belief that despite imago dei, the human condition is that we cannot reach this potential, because of original sin, is very flawed, because original sin as 'ontologically present' is difficult to still believe in a benevolent God, because if God is all loving then surely he would have not allowed human nature to be sinful and make human powers weakened and allow death. Additionally, he wanted woman to experience a painful labour 'I will make your pains in childbearing very severe', that is absolutely cruel, just because Eve disobeyed God once, surely people should be forgiven for their mistakes as that would be the most loving thing. Rousseau, for example argued that humans are by nature good and inclined to defend the weak and work for a better society. I strongly agree with this, because I believe we try our absolute hardest to cure and save ill people for example. Additionally, we try to build a more peaceful society, by bringing in laws that make everyone equal, for example, equal rights for women to vote, we are also trying very hard to get rid of discrimination and prejudices towards people with different faiths and cultures etc. However, the idea that we are by nature good is not always true, because terrorists, for example are not good they are going against everything that makes a peaceful civilised society and world, they are trying to destroy everything important. Although they are evil and sinful that does not mean they are naturally sinful, because I believe we are all born with no good or evil nature, it is the environment and the upbringing we experience that shapes if we are naturally good or not. This is why terrorists are evil, because their surroundings are at disharmony so they live in violence, hatred and a society of terror. It is impossible for them to be born evil, as Rousseau and Locke support this idea by saying the 'blank state' we are born with is neither good or evil state, but readiness to make free choices. This all highlights just how pessimistic Augustine's teaching on human nature is.

Good link to God's benevolence – philosophical problem of sin as ontological condition. Some good examples used here to develop candidate's argument that we do not have an essentially good or evil nature and therefore in this way, Augustine's understanding could be seen as pessimistic. Good scholarly links too.

Through Adam and Eve's disobedience the will is now divided. Through reason it knows what good is but is often motivated by concupiscence rather than goodness. Concupiscence is sexual lust but can also refer to other uncontrolled desires such as food money etc. It dominates the desiring aspect of the soul now that the will is divided. The will can be driven by cupiditas and caritas- selfish and generous love. Now the will is divided it is in conflict with knowing what is good but ends up doing what is not, motivated by desire. This is akrasia, a weakness of the will, the paradox of voluntarily choosing something to do something which we know is against our best interests 'It is no longer I myself who do it, but it is sin living in me', this is from St Pauls Letter to the Romans, where he shows that this inclination to be sinful comes somewhere else than Christ. To demonstrate the idea of akrasia Augustine used his example of a beautiful chaste woman to show continence, a self constraint. Not even the woman could convince Augustine to embrace celibacy "Lord, make me chaste, but not yet', this again supports my belief that Augustine's teaching on human nature is too pessimistic, because the idea that every single person's will is divided and is motivated by sexual desires seems very negative, we may have sexual desires but that is not what we are motivated by, there is much more we aim and desire to do, for example, achieve a great career, help the sick etc. It also seems very negative again because a lot of us choose to do something which is against our best interests, but in fact helps and benefits others, this surely is not a negative thing unlike what Augustine thinks of the divided will. For example, by sacrificing your life in a war, you are eliminating your chance of living your life further and leaving your family behind, however, you are doing it to help save your country and the futures of others. However, Augustine's idea of our uncontrolled sexual desire can be slightly more optimistic than pessimistic, because by drawing attention to the dangers of uncontrolled sexual behaviour you can see how societies restrict it. Recognising human imperfection might lead to more moral progress. However, I still think Augustine's idea of akrasia and divided will is very negative and again makes his teaching too pessimistic.

One or two points here not very clearly explained. Is this a good example of akrasia here? Akrasia (literally 'weakness of will') is doing something against our best interests, that we know is the wrong thing...whereas it could be argued a person sacrificing their life in a war knows through other means that he / she is doing the 'right thing'. Perhaps the candidate could unpick the difficulty of akrasia – is there really such a thing as a 'conflicted will' and could this have existed pre-Fall?

However, Freud, would disagree when talking about sexual desires, because he argues that libido is a vital and natural element of human development, sex is not just about reproduction but about the defining factor in human relations. He believes libido is again significantly important in the development of a person's personality. Here Augustine's teaching on human nature can be seen as slightly optimistic, because sex is an important part in relationships, which Freud agrees with. However, the problem is that his link between sex and transmission of sin makes sex only necessary for reproduction. Sex can transmit sexual disorders, but it is impossible to transmit sin. Sin is a product of our environment, for example, family and religion rather than a product of sexual intercourse. Augustine fails to acknowledge the natural enjoyment of sex within marriage. However, Freud disagrees with Augustine in terms of original sin being transmitted through sexual intercourse and that you can be redeemed by God's grace and faith, but he doesn't completely dismiss Augustine's psychological insights. For example, the psychological problems shown by his neurotic patients highlighted the fact that they can be traced back to a historical moment in their earlier life. Therefore, Freud, shares Augustine's view that human personality is not chosen by individual but is the result of history and environment. Freud also accepts that sexual neurosis can be transmitted through culture and society which is not too different from Augustine's idea of Original Sin being transmitted. His suggested remedy for neurosis and feelings of guilt is through psychoanalysis, very different from Augustine's which lies in hope and redemption from God's grace and faith. Psychoanalysis involves analysing the events in someone's life that led to the trauma and helping that person to live a happy life. I strongly agree with Freud's remedy much more than Augustine's, because it is much more realistic and positive, it logically works. Whereas, God's grace and faith only seems reasonable if you are a believer in God.

Therefore, for a Christian theist, perhaps Augustine's understanding offers optimism for redemption and oneness with God; whereas for those outside of God, it is pessimistic?

Augustine taught that the rebellious will could be overcome by God's grace and faith and then the summum bonum (supreme good) can be achieved. God elects those he knows will answer his love and be restored to paradise to be redeemed. The elected are those who believe in moving to a life of spiritual freedom beyond this life. This idea seems very unfair and the problem is it contradicts the New Testament that 'all' are saved by Jesus' sacrificing and God's redemption for everyone to achieve eternal life. The idea of election seems very pessimistic and does not coincide with the benevolent God. Unless perhaps this means that God saves across races and cultures. However, it still seems unfair and Edward Gibbon Scorns agrees, he argues that 'His learning is too often borrowed and his arguments too often his own", this implies that the authority of Augustine's work lies in using the Bible as an argument. I think using the Bible as a source of authority and argument does not count, because no one can certainly be sure that everything in the Bible is true, therefore, we cannot use it to construct an argument.

Sweeping statement and weak argument here – unless the candidate brings it around to assessing the effect of taking the Fall story in Genesis 3 literally...can Augustine still have meaning with a symbolic reading?

Additionally, even if the Bible is true, using it for an argument is not thinking up anything new and does not make your argument unique enough and therefore less persuasive. Augustine seems to take the Bible too literally and perhaps he could use the Bible to construct his argument but in a more metaphorical, symbolic way. However, although less unlikely in my opinion the Bible can in a way count as a source of argument, because it can support and make your argument stronger, because it is evidence in some people's opinions, however, I do not believe this is a strong enough point.

Rather vague. Candidate does not seem to know how to use Election and validity of the Bible to support his/her thread of argument here. Election is brought in but the material with the Bible is reflected on but to no end. The commentary here seems to serve to show off knowledge but there is nothing constructive done with it to serve an argument.

Only God knows who he will elect and is deserving of his grace to be rewarded with heaven then all humans can do is to persevere in hope and faith. In this way Augustine, can be seen as an optimist, because without God's grace no one would be saved from the effects of Original Sin. However, Augustine's view undermines the Christian belief in the God of love and the sacrifice of Christ for all the 'sins of the world' not for the sins of a few, which many of his contemporaries also criticised him for this. However, God's grace and faith can make Augustine's teaching on human nature slightly less pessimistic, because maybe it offers a solution. The Fall is a symbol of a spiritual journey which reminds us of social responsibility, which is very positive. Augustine's teaching again can be viewed in a slight optimistic light if you interpret Augustine today, the Fall can be seen as I just said a symbol of a person's spiritual journey. Renewal and redemption are positive symbols of the spiritual and psychological life. Many Christians today consider creation, Fall and redemption as the history of each person's individual life. Referring back to predestination and and election again, the problem with this again is if our fates are already decided, what responsibility can we have with our moral actions, we cannot do good in our life if it is already decided for us. If we have no real freedom, what incentive do we have to become better?

This would fit in with Election. Good discussion of the question fulfils the criterion of 'engagement'.

However, I still believe Augustine's teaching on human nature is fairly pessimistic, because of how irrational and dangerous it is. This supports Dawkins belief who argues that the Christian notion of the Fall and Original Sin is not completely contrary to evolutionary biology, however, is still absurd and dangerous. He argues that it is absurd to imagine that the corruption of human nature lies completely on two individuals' one mistake. Evolutionary biology supports the idea that Augustine is wrong, because it shows that we created from less sophisticated animal forms who did not have the kind of consciousness which made them actively rebel. Therefore, a literal belief in Adam and Eve makes no sense. I strongly agree with this, because life in this world is constantly changing, it is in flux and is steadily becoming more diverse. This supports Heraclitus who believes no man can 'step in the same river twice', the world is in constant flux. Evolution sees life on earth as moving closer to 'perfection', becoming better adapted to its environment. Dawkins also states that even a symbolic account of The Fall does not eliminate Christianity's obsession with guilt, sex etc. I agree with this, however, the symbolic account of the Fall does contain important truths about state of humanity, which is very positive and important, for example, it highlights the idea of social responsibility. Lastly, Dawkins argues that the idea that God should wish to restore humanity by killing Jesus on the cross is irrational and sadomasochistic. I agree with this and also the idea that humanity will be restored by killing Jesus is crazy and impossible, the only way humanity can be restored is by creating a harmonious and peaceful society.

Steven Pinker also shares Dawkins views. He talks about the humanitarian principle and his argument is that religion in general, and Christianity in particular has been responsible for suffering and the degradation of humanity until Post-Enlightenment when the irrational superstitions of Christianity such as the Fall, Grace and Original Sin were replaced with the humanitarian principle. The principle is the idea that humans get on better with each other when each person takes into account the interests of others. The challenge highlights just how much trouble religion causes, perhaps if there was none, the world would be a much more peaceful and civilised place. I also highly agree with this, because it highlights how we do not need God's grace, we can reason ourselves to perfection, because we are autonomous beings. Therefore, this highlights just how wrong in my opinion and pessimistic Augustine's teaching on human nature is.

However, Niebuhr would disagree he supports Augustine a lot. He argues that by rejecting the notion of sin we as humans are failing to realise that no action can never be entirely good and this causes greater injustices and more suffering. This may not be apparent at an individual level but collectively when people act in groups their mistakes become exaggerated. Niebuhr accuses both religious and non-religious leaders of ignorance if they think the power of reason and belief in moral goodness brings about a just and fair society. He may agree with Augustine in terms of sin but he does not argue so strongly about it, he believes original sin is both 'inevitable but not necessary', sin is apparent in evil as well as good acts. Evil people can do good things and good people can still selfishly desire self-affirmation. Another difference from Niebuhr to Augustine is Niebuhr does believe there is a remedy to human condition, it is for the human ego to understand its own nature fully by coming into a proper relationship with God and is then able to realise both its realisations and possibilities. Niebuhr's views are much more optimistic than Augustine's, however, I still do not agree with them. This is because, I believe that there are some actions that are wholly good, for example, carrying out cardiopulmonary resuscitation (CPR) you are saving someone's life which is a very positive thing, there is nothing bad or sinful about that action, if you did not carry out CPR then that would be a sinful act. However, from Niebuhr's beliefs Augustine can be seen as realistic, not pessimistic. Even if the Fall did not happen Augustine can perhaps be seen to give a realistic take on human nature and corruption, even if we do not like the reality. However, I believe this is more wrong than right, I think Augustine is more pessimistic than realistic, there may be a lot of bad in human nature but there is more good.

Overall I think Augustine's teaching on human nature is pessimistic but not 'too pessimistic', if you consider God's grace, faith and the idea that Augustine is slightly realistic. However, even if Augustine is slightly realistic that still does not deny his pessimism. Dawkins, for example, I especially agree with, however, Niebuhr I do not. It is extremely difficult to view Augustine's teaching on human nature as optimistic even if you do take into account some of his realism views.

AO1: Level 4 (10 marks)

This answer contains a wealth of subject knowledge, a range of scholarly views and evidence and excellent specialist vocabulary. The candidate makes good attempts to address the question throughout. The reason this answer is limited, and does not quite reach level 5, is because the material needs to be 'used appropriately'. Although this was achieved 'on the whole', there were times when material was used but not assessed effectively as part of building an argument. The candidate has seemed to want to show off as much as he/ she knows about Augustine but needs to be a bit more selective if he/ she is to build a coherent argument. Some repetition in places.

AO2: Level 5 (20 marks)

This answer just met the criteria for a level 5 because there is a good range of scholarly views and the candidate does state his/her views clearly, with some development and justification. Analysis is generally successful. However, it is bottom level 5 because the argument often lacks clarity and the quantity of material detracts from building a sustained argument.

Overall 30/40 75% Grade B

Exercise: *How convincing is Augustine's teaching about the Fall and Original Sin?* Write a five paragraph essay plan on this essay title. remember to unpack and fully discuss the non-technical word 'convincing'. If you wish to introduce a more optimistic view, then use Aquinas and his view of synderesis. (Synoptic links - Natural Law ethics and conscience sections of the Ethics paper).

To what extent can Jesus be regarded as no more than a teacher of wisdom? (40/40 Grade A* OCR June 2018)

In order to determine the extent to which Jesus was solely a teacher of wisdom, other roles which he purportedly held (e.g. as a spiritual leader, a historical figure or a revolutionary) must also be considered. Arguably, however, Jesus was most likely a historical, revolutionary figure - given the nature of many biblical accounts.

A good, brief introduction which also indicates a thesis – that Jesus was a revolutionary figure (in a political sense) rather than divine Son of God.

Firstly, to consider perhaps the most widely acknowledged interpretation - was Jesus a religious leader, the son of God? Despite an irrefutable lack of hard, verifiable evidence concerning the more supernatural events of Jesus' life (e.g. the resurrection, the ascension, turning water to wine,) professor of theology Marcus Borg suggests that: 'If we understand these stories as parables about Jesus — as metaphorical narratives about him — then the question of their factuality vanishes as an important question.' Although, the reverse is arguably true - without some innate divinity, the character of Jesus ceases to exist. That is, to take away his relationship with God would not leave him as a mere 'moral teacher' or 'revolutionary' but instead, as a maniac. A notion presented most concisely by C.S. Lewis: 'A man who was merely a man and said the sort of things Jesus said would not be a great moral teacher. He would either be a lunatic - on a level with the man who says he is a poached egg – or else he would be the Devil of Hell.' Hence, Jesus' teachings and his being the son of God are indivisible. One must then decide, if still disregarding any religious significance, Jesus was aware of this falsehood (i.e. was a liar,) or not. It is most illogical to suggest that Jesus was some great deceiver, for it would render him both a hypocrite ('Do not lie to each other,' Colossians 3:9) and a moron (as maintaining such a falsehood resulted in crucifixion.) The idea that Jesus believed himself to be the son of God, but was mistaken, may then seem most probable - but in a society which was so fanatically monotheistic? Would it not be more sensical to preach to the choir, to deliver such dogma to a more welcoming Greek or Egyptian society (i.e. one which is polytheistic)? Again, this certainly calls Jesus' sanity into account. But there seems a great juxtaposition in a man who is able to simultaneously deliver such profound teachings (on an afterlife, on morality and on human nature) yet is unable to realise his own instabilities and delusions. Having said that, it is still important to weigh the likelihood of Jesus' divinity against other commonplace alternatives - as a historical figure, a revolutionary or a teacher of wisdom.

The paragraph is rather long – paragraphing is important because it suggests analytical structure. Nonetheless, this candidate has a very good analytical style, using terms and concepts such as 'juxtaposition' and excellent rhetorical questions. Despite what some teachers say, rhetorical questions suggest probing analysis (as long as they are also answered) but even if unanswered they suggest evaluation. Religious leader and divine Son of God are not the same thing – of course, the question is begged what does 'divine

Son of God' mean? Is there biblical evidence for this claim? How has the church interpreted this claim?

If Jesus of Nazareth is a mere historical figure, then, the origin of the term 'Son of God' must remain significant to biblical scholars, for it is arguably the reason knowledge of his existence has endured. Perhaps it is symbolic of Jesus' importance on a personal level to his followers, something generated post-death to discuss his impact (likewise with terms such as 'Lord,' or 'Messiah.') It is also important to mention that any discussions around the historicity of Jesus are more-or-less in vain, as scholars have now reached a consensus on the matter. As professor Bart Ehrman puts it: 'These views are so extreme and so unconvincing to 99.99 percent of the real experts that anyone holding them is as likely to get a teaching job in an established department of religion as a six-day creationist is likely to land one in a bona fide department of biology.'

I don't think this paragraph adds very much of substance to the main thesis – apart from a rather clever but unexplained quotation.

Indeed, both his baptism and crucifixion are recorded by independent, non-Christian historians of the era -thereby allowing them to be generally accepted as historical fact. First, by Jewish historian Josephus in his 'Antiquities of the Jews,' written around 93-94 A.D. And later, by Roman senator and historian Tacitus in 'Annals' (an account of Roman history) in around 110-120 A.D. Given the often critical nature of these texts, it is unlikely that they were doctored/forged by a Christian writer. Furthermore, other 'criterions' can be used to verify/discredit the authenticity of historical events, criterions which too can be applied to

114

the life of Jesus. For example, the 'criterion of embarrassment' (i.e. it is unlikely the Gospels would fabricate such a humiliating death for Jesus,) the 'criterion of coherence' (i.e. it is consistent with the historical context,) the 'criterion of rejection' (i.e. it has not been disputed by other historical accounts of the time,) and the 'criterion of attestation' (i.e. it is derived from multiple sources.) The Gospels, given their subjectivity, cannot be used in the same way - to scrutinise the 'historical Jesus,' Jesus of Nazareth, but are nonetheless important in considering his character, so long as they are taken with enough scepticism.

Notice how this candidate uses analytical words and phrases throughout (see my list in an appendix at the back of this book). Analytical words and phrases represent an empirical test of good analytical and evaluative writing. Examples in this paragraph are 'indeed' (for emphasis), 'furthermore' (suggesting a point is being pushed further) and 'for example' (suggesting a point is being grounded), and 'nonetheless' suggesting a qualifying contrast (a bit like the word 'but'). Notice the high quality of well-illustrated analysis in this paragraph. The next paragraph starts with the link word 'hence'.

Hence, given the certainty of Jesus' existence as a historical figure, it is the nature of his existence (e.g. as a teacher of wisdom, a revolutionary or the Son of God) which is most valuable to debate. In particular, there is an emerging demographic of 'Christian Atheism,' those who abide by the ethical code laid out by Jesus, but reject Christianity's supernatural claims. Arguably, this theological position can trace its roots back to Ludwig Wittgenstein - a great Austrian philosopher, who regarded Jesus not as some abstract being but as the embodiment of spiritual and moral livelihood. Symbolically, this moral teaching is epitomised in Jesus' Sermon on the Mount, almost in imitation of Moses' preaching of the Ten Commandments on Mount Sinai. In Matthew 5:19 - 'Therefore, whoever breaks one of the least of these commandments, and teaches others to do the same so, will be called least in the kingdom of heaven.' Of course, this is maintained throughout the New Testament through Jesus' use of parables, proverbs and examples. Or more explicitly in the Gospel of Mark (10:17): 'Good teacher, what must I do to inherit eternal life?' Significantly though, this interpretation of Jesus is compatible both with his historical figure and the supernatural, divine one detailed in the Gospels. For some scholars, this is essential if Christianity wishes to engage in constructive dialogue with other other major religions. For example, John Hick argues that by regarding Jesus as a moral teacher first and foremost, other great teachers of wisdom, 'gifts to the world' (e.g. Buddha, Muhammad, Moses) can be more readily used in conjunction with Christianity. To some extent, this is still problematic though, as denying Jesus' divinity is to negate any moral authority he may have held, thereby placing him on level terms with all other teachers of wisdom.

An evaluation is introduced here halfway through the paragraph, where the candidate uses the phrase 'significantly though' to indicate an important evaluative link with the twin ideas of historicity of Christ and supernatural interpretation of his 'sonship'. Further problems are also indicated in the paragraph (the candidate signals this with the phrase 'this is problematic though').

Finally, one must consider Jesus' role as a liberator, a revolutionary. Having lived in Roman-occupied territory for the majority of his life, much of this revolves around Jesus' political engagement. The extent to which he partook in the upheaval of class/social structures of the era is important to modern-day Christians as it exemplifies the extent to which they should become politically involved. Albeit, the majority of this involvement is typically 'creative non-violent resistance' (e.g. from Matthew 5 - 'If anyone slaps you on the right cheek, turn to them the other cheek also,' 'And if anyone would sue you and take your tunic, let him have your cloak as well.') That is, the ingenious acts which both demonstrate defiance whilst passively humiliating those in opposition. But there is also clear biblical evidence to the contrary, of Jesus' more active revolutionary nature. Most notably in Matthew 5:12, 'He overturned the tables of the money changers and the seats of those selling doves.' Moreover, liberation theologists highlight Jesus' preferential treatment of the poor and of the marginalised (e.g. in healing the Centurion's servant, in the parable of the 'Good Samaritan' and in treating lepers, prostitutes and other such social outcasts.) Such behaviour has led some theologians to believe Jesus was aligned with the Zealots - a group wishing to incite hatred and contempt towards the Roman empire, in the hopes that it may be driven from the Holy Land. A view discussed in S.G.F Brandon's divisive 'Jesus and the Zealots,' which suggests Jesus was a politically-motivated 'freedom fighter' before several Gospel passages were rewritten to paint him in a more pacifistic light. What is more clear though, throughout the synoptic Gospels, is that Jesus sought to remove class disparities - indeed, amongst his very disciples were the 'unclean'/'am ha'aretz' fishermen, tax collector (Matthew) and zealot (Simon.) It is this pursuit of liberty, be it political or spiritual, that has persisted and from which the oppressed in Latin America drew inspiration in the civil wars of the 1970s-90s.

First class scholarly analysis of the argument for a political interpretation of Christ. Notice the excellent use of scholars and highly relevant quotations to support the case that Jesus was crucified for being a trouble maker to both Romans and the ruling Jewish High Priestly group.

In conclusion, it is both a drastic understatement and a flaw in logic to say that Jesus should be regarded as a 'teacher of wisdom' and no more. Unequivocally, he must have been an influential historical figure, but to a great extent, a liberator and a revolutionary too.

Excellent concise conclusion which follows from the preceding analysis and backs up the thesis statement in the opening paragraph. This is a powerful full mark answer and an excellent example of analytical and evaluative writing.

AO1 Knowledge and Understanding Level 6 (16 marks)

An excellent attempt to address the question showing understanding and engagement with the material; excellent ability to select and deploy relevant information. Extensive range of scholarly views, academic approaches, and/or sources of wisdom and authority are used to demonstrate knowledge and understanding.

AO2 Analysis, evaluation and application. Level 6 (24 marks)

An excellent demonstration of analysis and evaluation in response to the question. Confident and insightful critical analysis and detailed evaluation of the issue. Views skilfully and clearly stated, coherently developed and justified. Excellent line of reasoning, well-developed and sustained, which is coherent, relevant and logically structured.

Overall 40/40 Grade A*

Exercise: Identify two scholars you might use in this debate about the divine status of Jesus Christ. Write one paragraph supporting the thesis that Jesus was divine and one against. Then write a nuanced conclusion evaluating both views and coming down on one side or the other.

'Theological pluralism undermines Christian belief.' Discuss. (39/40 Grade A*)

As a theological pluralist believes that Christianity is but one path of salvation among many, is it really possible to accept that the two words 'Christian' and 'pluralist' can go together? Or, can pluralists who call themselves Christian be seen as having left the historic Christian faith in favour of a new form of spirituality which has nothing to do with the Bible, the creeds and the views of the Church? This essay will make the case that pluralism actually strengthens Christian belief, when the term 'belief' is defined more broadly than 'dogma' to include the ideas of faith and experience. It will do this by exploring the views of John Hick who sees the foundations of pluralism as in religious experience and contrasting these with inclusivist and exclusivist approaches to salvation and truth.

Superb opening paragraph. Notice the candidate uses one entirely valid approach to essay-writing, that of interrogating the question to try to underneath the sub-issues which underly it. Some teachers tell students never to ask questions in an essay. That's bad advice.

It could be argued that pluralism has nothing to do with Christianity because the major denominations of the Church agree on the doctrine of Council of Chalcedon in 451CE that Christ is unique among all humans – and all religions – for being the incarnation of God, one person with two natures, human and divine. Belief in Jesus as the God-Man is found widely across denominations in theology, statements of faith and hymnody (consider the words of 'O Come All Ye Faithful'). Furthermore, Jesus Christ came to offer salvation through his death on the cross to all human beings (I John 2:2). Therefore, to say that other religions offer a path of salvation is to deny Jesus' universal status and thus, to deny the most important doctrine of Christianity. This is, in fact, heresy and explains why pluralism has been officially condemned by the Roman Catholic Church as well as by the majority of Protestant Church bodies.

Interesting paragraph employing a historical argument about the Council of Chalcedon. However, over the Enlightenment period a liberal version of Christianity has emerged that argues for many paths to the same God. An extreme version of this is John Hick's universal pluralism.

The idea that Christian faith rests on the Chalcedonian formulation ignores the fact that many people were considered to have been Christians prior to 451CE. The Bible contains no clear statement of the 'two natures' and therefore it may be wrong to make this doctrine the standard for all Christians to believe. In addition to this, the doctrine of the two natures has never been explained – it is merely an assertion of the Church, a compromise in a larger and complicated philosophical discussion that may have surprised the historical Jesus.

John Hick says that there is an alternative way to think of Jesus than the 'two-natures' approach. Jesus could be considered someone who achieved a very high degree of God-consciousness, so much so that he became an example and inspiration for others. This means that a Christian can be led to God through Jesus without having to believe, literally, in the creeds. A Christian can therefore be open to the idea that figures in other religions could have achieved God/Reality consciousness. What makes them a Christian rather than, for example, a Buddhist, is not the uniqueness of their doctrine, but the fact that they came to a deeper understanding of life through Jesus rather than through the Buddha. If 'belief' is thought of in terms of experience rather than doctrine, then Christianity would not be undermined – according to Hick.

John Hick seems to abandon any reference to Christ preferring a vaguer idea of a deity. This raises the question - is universalism incompatible with Christianity rather than some version of deism. More could be said on Hick here, and Hick should be throughly criticised and evaluated.

Of course, Christians who believe in the historic creeds could reply that while Chalcedon's views may not be explicit in the Gospels, they are implicit – these ideas grew out of the real experience of the disciples with the miraculous life of Jesus. Therefore, it is no mere accident that it became a central doctrine of Christianity. Furthermore, the fact that Hick uses terms like 'Ultimate Reality', 'divine reality', and 'transcendent reality' alongside the term 'God' means that he has really departed from Christianity and its more definite view of a Trinitarian God.

That's a better paragraph as evaluation is beginning to show.

The Catholic Church, for example, believes that there is a direct path from the Bible to church traditions and traditional beliefs about the nature of Jesus. For centuries ideas about salvation were expressed in an 'exclusivistic' way ('extra Ecclesiam nulla salus' - outside the church no salvation), though more recently theologians such as Karl Rahner have accounted for the fact that there are God-fearing individuals outside of the 'household of faith' in both the Old Testament and New Testament (Rahner spoke about those who worship the 'unknown God' in Acts 17; there is also Jethro, the Centurion at the cross, and others) so that is it more accurate to say that God 'includes' in the salvation of Jesus even those outside the church who are faithful to the truth that they know. He calls these 'anonymous Christians' to indicate that they are considered by God as Christian even though they are not aware of this. Of course inclusivism, like exclusivism, is centred on the belief in Jesus as the unique God-Man who saves the world.

Good paragraph which introduces sound knowledge of Rahner - another important scholar on this subject.

John Hick raises several challenges to these viewpoints. First, there are issues with the miraculous beliefs about Jesus' life according to modern historical research. However, to focus only on these questions is to miss the fact that belief in the miraculous nature of Jesus is an expression of how important Jesus was to the disciples. Jesus opened up for them an experience of reality that was new, a less self-centered way of life that utterly changed them, gave them purpose and a sense of mission about sharing the love of God. Surely it is this experience that is at the heart of Christianity? In terms of having a more vague view of God, isn't it true that God is a mystery? So, to define the word 'God' precisely would mean that we are turning God into an object of human enquiry.

Furthermore, if we say that an experience is at the heart of Christianity, then Christianity is more about having an authentic experience rather than believing in the 'right things'. In fact, Christianity should be thought of in this way: individuals who are inspired by Jesus to have less of a self-centred life and more of a God-centred life. This person comes to know Jesus through their encounter with scripture, tradition and the Christian community – but it is not these things, but their experience, that should remain central.

After all, isn't so much discord in the world the result of experience being hardened into teaching which then becomes further hardened into absolute doctrines? This then leads to people feeling 'right' and seeing others as 'wrong' which, in turn, fuels hatred, segregation and violence. We would all be better off, says Hick, by basing Christianity on our experience of Jesus and being open to the idea that those in other religions can have equally valid experiences which can also lead to less self-centred lives.

Good development of Hick's view (which comes from his experience as a priest) that the essence of religion is how we live our lives in reflection of universal divine attributes (such as love and justice).

Of course, Christians who root their beliefs in the Bible and tradition may object that this way of thinking can lead to an 'anything goes' philosophy. For instance, does this mean that all religions are automatically 'good'? What about a religion that worships the devil and engages in all sorts of anti-humanitarian practices? Furthermore, the religious pluralist ignores that there are other Christian paths that can recognise goodness and wisdom in other religions – as well as hope that non-Christians will also make it to heaven. These paths do not require that Christians surrender what is truly unique about their religions, the incarnation of the God-Man Jesus.

Good AO2 points here showing evaluation of the pluralist's position. The candidate might consider the Bible's teaching on this issue. Much hangs on how we interpret verses such as Jesus' statement in John that he is 'the way, the truth and the life'. In the next paragraph the candidate mentions 'assumptions', but it's our assumptions about Scripture that explains the divisions in the churches on the issue of pluralism.

However, there are a number of assumptions in these points that the pluralist could take issue with. First, Hick does not believe that his views are relativistic: you can judge a religion, but not on its doctrines alone. Rather, they can be judged on how well they enable people to be less egocentric. Therefore, a religion which has anti-humanitarian practices can be judged as less God/Reality centred than other religions. Furthermore, an inclusivist approach can be seen as patronising: 'you have some truth, but I have more and better truth'. Is that really an attitude that is in line with the biblical mandate to love our neighbours?

The question here is an entirely valid way of evaluating as it casts doubt on the central proposition.

In conclusion, it has to be recognised that most churches simply do not consider it possible to be a Christian and a religious pluralist. However, this does not mean that there are not religious pluralists sitting on the pews in those churches. Therefore, the reality 'on the ground' may be different than official Church views. When the word 'belief' is defined merely in terms of traditional dogma then, certainly, Christian pluralism can be argued to undermine Christian belief. However, when belief is seen to include the idea of 'faith' and the kinds of experiences that lead to an inspired and ethical life, then pluralism actually can be seen to strengthen Christian belief.

Excellent conclusion. Generally a thorough and interesting essay. As it happens, the Church of England embraces all positions from liberal inclusivist to evangelical exclusivist. It's an interesting issue which is a more credible stance in a world that is clearly pluralistic. I like the way the essay sets up a tension between historical Christianity in the Chalcedonian formula (a fifth century Church council) and the liberalism of Hick. Teachers disagree about whether it's appropriate to use questions in an essay - my view is it makes for rigorous interrogation of the issues underpinning a question. See the summary of the examiner's comments on the 2018 at the end of the book.

AO1 level 6 (15 marks)

AO2 level 6 (24 marks)

Overall 39/40 Grade A*

Exercise: Make up your own exam question on pluralism after studying the specification carefully. Then write an opening paragraph on yoru won question that sets up a tension between two scholars or two scholarly views (in the essay above it is the view of the council of Chalcedon in 451 versus John Hick).

Critically compare Daly's and Ruether's teaching on God (34/40, Grade A)

Fundamentally, both Ruether and Daly are trying to promote and subsequently rectify the same issue of gender inequality within Christianity. However, they have rather different perspectives and approaches to the issue as, while Ruether focuses on reforming the Church to make it less patriarchal and sexist, Daly holds a more radical and extremist view and is seeking total female dominance. With regard to their teachings on God, it is evident that there are various similarities as they both ultimately disagree with the fact that God is referenced in male terms, yet on a more specific level they have different goals when it comes to the future of the Church and its teachings on God.

Good introductory paragraph that hints at major similarities and differences between them. Note the command words 'critically compare' - we need to think carefully how we 'critically' compare, rather than just point to differences. Both scholars started life as Roman Catholics.

Firstly, Ruether takes issue with the idea that God is male and believes that this has allowed for the institutionalisation of patriarchy within the Church. According to her, the Church has lost its egalitarian roots as by saying 'God the father' patriarchy is denoted and this seems unjust for women. Instead, Ruether teaches that we must also address God using some feminine language and she supports this with scripture as often there is the idea of the Goddess as the source of life. For instance, in Isaiah, God is depicted as a Mother going through childbirth as it says "now I will cry out like a woman in labour". Furthermore, Ruether claims that there is this concept of 'Sophia' in the Holy Spirit as a form of Wisdom, adding to the need for a female aspect of God. This is somewhat similar to Daly's teaching on God as she believes that a male God has been used to justify the marginalisation and mistreatment of women in the Church and as such this view of God must be changed. However, Daly takes it one step further in that she believes that God must be castrated and cannot not be referred to in either male or female terms, but rather replaced with an authentic human existence. She uses terms like "the transvaluation of Christianity" and "female be-ing" to suggest that there is no need for an objective God, and in removing him, women will have more power within society. From this, it seems evident that the key difference between these two feminists stems from their diverse attitudes towards men as generally Ruether seeks equality while Daly sees women as the better sex. This is an important criticism of Daly as her teachings on God can be seen to be too exclusive and biased as it promotes lesbian separatism. As a result, one could argue that Ruether's approach is more reasonable as it acknowledges the need for male and female co-operation.

Good detailed AO1 knowledge here. Synoptic links could be made to the person of Christ as liberator - the one who touched lepers and generally sided with outcasts.

One of Daly's prominent teachings on God is that he forcibly impregnated the Virgin Mary who is "the total rape" victim. For Daly, this image has legitimised the abuse of women by the Church over the centuries. In addition, she had the view that God had been used to justify the destruction of women's spiritual nature and as such we must break free from this self-imposed cultural imprisonment of religion. Daly puts emphasis on the fact that only women possess the ability to remove these false ideas about God, and refers to it as the Apollonian veil which prevents people from accomplishing their creativity and imagination. This is quite dissimilar to Ruether who argued that theological language referring to God must be based on the apophatic assumption that God is beyond language and therefore gender. Yet, often theologians tend to use male-gendered language to emphasise God's transcendence and female language to emphasise God's immanence. So, while we can use gendered language in analogies and symbols of how humans experience God, Ruether promotes the overall use of more inclusive language. However, it is evident that Ruether did not always stick to this idea as she was more partial to the idea of a Goddess which would compromise the sovereignty of God and reduce the credibility of her teachings. Furthermore, one could argue that she over analyses the situation and perhaps she is making more of an issue than there needs to be.

The candidate needs to remember refer back to the question and make explicit the critical comments.

Another key teaching on God comes from Ruether and addresses the concept of whether or not a male saviour can save women. On the one hand, she argues that with Jesus (the Word of God/Logos) being historically male, women would have to adapt to a male mindset in order to be saved. Similarly, Jesus was promoted as a triumphal king and as a result Churches felt justified in only having male officials who could represent this figure. On the other hand, Ruether believes that salvation was available to women once radical tradition is rediscovered as she suggests that the maleness of Jesus isn't relevant. According to her, we should view Jesus as simply a ruler who sought to restore all human relations, particularly focusing on the marginalised which included women at that time. As a result, it seems clear that Ruether was more interested in how Christianity could be reformed to cater for women. This isn't quite the case for Daly who saw little benefit in reforming the Church as she completely rejects the Catholic Church as fundamentally sexist and patriarchal. This is another key difference between their teachings on God as they have different visions for the future of Christianity.

A link could be made of Simone de Beauvoir's influence on Ruether.

In conclusion, while both feminist theologians are looking to remove the gender inequality within the Church, they have rather different views on how this should be accomplished. They both highlight the idea that in order to gain this social change they need to use extreme measures, however perhaps in Daly's case this has lead to the distortion of her message. Overall, it would seem that Ruether's approach is more equipped to bring about a change in Christianity regarding equality whereas Daly's approach is somewhat irrational in the way she demonises men, alienating them, which ultimately seems counterproductive.

Critical comparison is slightly 'added on' at the end here. Perhaps as a tactic it may be better to have three areas of critical comparison in view in the opening paragraph, which are then fully evaluated in the bulk of the essay. The final paragraph could then be used to sum up the elements of this critical comparison - back to my initial point, that to compare is descriptive and to 'critically compare' is evaluative.

AO1 Level 6 (14 marks)

AO2 Level 5 (20 marks)

Overall 34/40 85% Grade A

Exercise: rewrite the opening paragraph to make clear three areas of critical comparison between Daly and Ruether, and the broad thesis of the essay.

To what extent are Bonhoeffer's teachings still relevant today? (29/40, Grade B, OCR, June 2018)

Dietrich Bonhoeffer was a theologian in the second world war who abandoned his previous ideas, namely that of secular pacifism, to fight the threat of Nazi Germany. His theology was one of action, truly embodying Christian morals, which ultimately got him executed by the Nazis. His theology today is still used, however, its application and effectiveness can be difficult in today's society.

Slightly overstates Bonhoeffer's role. His involvement with the Stauffenberg bomb lot of 1944 was very marginal. His protest was rather more about establishing a community which refused to compromise with Nazism and set up networks of support for those persecuted by the Nazis.

Possibly the biggest issue with the use of Bonhoeffer in today's society is that there is no singular threat to society, such as Hitler, instead threats are multi-faceted (Wilkinson), such as global warming, terrorism and capitalism. Bonhoeffer fled to America in fear of being called up to Germany's army, yet it was here in America that he realised he must return to Germany. Bonhoeffer was a pacifist, yet developed this term secular pacifist which meant a false non-belief in pacifism due to our secular ways. Bonhoeffer, as a Christian, struggled with this idea of violence, especially civil disobedience and tyrannicide. He viewed there to be no rational justification for civil disobedience, as the Bible often spoke against it. Tyrannicide which is the deliberate killing of a tyrant for the greater good (Wilkinson) he struggled with especially. However, Bonhoeffer was able to justify this involvement in these actions due to his faith in the 'grace of God'. A Christian may be able to use Bonhoeffer's theology taking in this aspect as a reason to disobey the state, although there is a risk that some people may take this idea too far, and extreme views may develop. Therefore as there is no single threat for our society to target, and the use of civil disobedience may be misinterpreted, Bonhoeffer's theology is of little use to today's society.

Arguably the greatest threat to Christianity today is consumerism and obsession with self. Bonhoeffer's teaching of costly grace and his belief in the formation of a new community still has much to teach us - but arguably Christians are as consumerist as anybody.

However, Bonhoeffer's push for truth pragmatically may be helpful in today's politics and society. Bonhoeffer disagreed with the German church at the time, as Hitler was abusing and manipulating the church to achieve his own goals. Bonhoeffer therefore joined the confessing church, which believed that you did not have to be from the Aryan race to join the church. They also believed that Christ is the only true authority for the church. This could be relevant today as liberation theologians wish to adopt Bonhoeffer's focus on Jesus as a leader and liberator. This is positive as it keeps in focus the uniqueness of Christianity which is that of Jesus Christ. This stems from Bonhoeffer's idea of a 'rusty sword', which are the outworn ethical attitudes of the church. This idea could be relevant to wider Christians as they look to return back to the essence of

Christianity. Although Christians must be careful not to remove all the church tradition, as this is what has helped bring Christianity to where it is today. These ideas of the search for the truth and good despite going against popular question may be of immense value today, and could be used in today's society.

Good focus on the question.

Finally Bonhoeffer did believe that eventually all Jews should convert to Christianity so that they are saved by God's grace. This exclusivist view may not fit modern times. However, Bonhoeffer did gain sympathy for the Jews' battles against the Nazis later in his life. He was even sent to prison for helping Jews escape to Switzerland. This care for our neighbours is an important aspect of his theology that can be of value in today's society.

Good example of practical (and non-violent) action.

To conclude, parts of Bonhoeffer's theology can be used in today's society. His pragmatic search for the truth, and care for those outside his religion should be learnt from. However, no longer are we fighting against one evil force, Hitler, in Bonhoeffer's case. Because of this much of Bonhoeffer's theology is difficult to apply today. Ultimately, what is most important about Bonhoeffer is summarised by Edmund Burke when he said: "the only thing necessary for the triumph of evil is for good mean to do nothing". This signifies how Bonhoeffer was a good man when he spoke out against evil, not just because of his religion, but also because it was his duty.

Well-argued essay but this lacks enough focus on Bonhoeffer's theology. The candidate needed to bring in concepts such as costly grace contained In Bonhoeffer's work The Cost of Discipleship. A quote from this book would help. There isn't enough evidence that the candidate has researched Bonhoeffer's theology - and seems to rely on one of the textbooks. Much better to read some fo Bonhoeffer for yourself. It's not worth referencing textbooks - only original sources and scholars.

AO1 Level 5 12 marks

A very good attempt to address the question demonstrating knowledge and understanding. Very good selection of relevant material, technical terms mostly accurate. a very good range of scholarly views, academic approaches, and/or sources of wisdom and authority are used to demonstrate knowledge and understanding

AO 2 Level 5 17 marks

A very good demonstration of analysis and evaluation in response to the question. successful and clear analysis, evaluation and argument. Views very well stated, coherently developed and justified. There is a well–developed and sustained line of reasoning which is coherent, relevant and logically structured.

Overall 29/40 Grade B

Exercise: *"Bonhoeffer's most significant teaching is on leadership",* *Discuss.* Write a five paragraph essay plan on this title, making sure to include evaluative comments that satisfy the AO2 criteria for level 6.

Insights

The examiners' report of 2018 complained of a lack of insight in many answers (AO2 criterion), and a lack of original research. I have produced a list of ideas which might help to trigger your own original research and insight. We need also to remember this is one holistic specification and there are many crosslinks between subjects in the three papers. So-called 'synoptic links' are to be encouraged - they show insight and originality.

Philosophy of Religion H573/1

Plato and Aristotle - The Platonic world of the Forms seems to connect with Kant's idea of an inaccessible noumenal realm (Ethics).

Aristotle's idea that everything has a true purpose or final cause influences Aquinas' natural law ethic where our purpose is to apply our human reason to live a flourishing life (eudaimonia).

Mind, body, soul dualism - seems to influence our view of life after death as many still believe the soul separates from the body at death. Arguably the Bible suggests both a physical resurrection (1 Corinthians 18) and a separation of soul and body (Luke 23:43).

Teleological argument - concerns design. Dawkins' evolutionary theory emphasises 'no purpose' but isn't the survival gene 'purposive', echoing the natural law precept of preservation of life in ethics?

Religious experience - our experiences of love, truth and beauty are all internal and unverifiable. But does this mean they are delusional (as some, such as Freud in Future of an Illusion suggest religious experiences are?)

Problem of evil - the inconsistent triad of God's omnipotence, omnibenevolence and omniscience seems to be unanswerable until we introduce free will. But does Augustine's account of the Fall of Humankind upset the free will defence (see Christian Thought section 1)?

Attributes of God - Boethius' defence of God's timelessness is a subtle argument defending God against the inconsistent triad. But does it work?

Religious language - ancient (negative, analogical, symbolic). Research the anaphatic and cataphatic ways (see the glossary of key terms at the back of this book).

Religious language - twentieth century. Wittgenstein's theory of language-games permits us to speak of metaphysical concepts like 'God 'or 'love'. Metaphysics cannot be killed off as easily as A J Ayer and his logical positivism suggests.

Ethics H573/2

Utilitarianism - does Mill's rule utilitarian collapse into act utilitarianism because whenever we face a moral dilemma we have to revert to being act utilitarians? Does utilitarianism ultimately fail because we are so poor at predicting consequences (but does it work fine for evaluating social policy because then we can look backwards?).

Situation Ethics - as agape is the highest form of love (and is impartial between friend and stranger) does it prove to be too demanding in practice because of the level of impartiality required?

Natural law - may have more flexibility than is often suggested because secondary precepts are not absolute (they depend on circumstances) and because of the principle of double effect.

Kantian ethics - paradoxically, we may be happier following Kantian categoricals because they do not require the level of judgement (guesswork) of consequentialist theories like utilitarianism and situation ethics. We also protect our integrity.

Euthanasia - seems to happen whether we like it or not as people near death and doctors employ double effect - they eliminate pain but unintentionally kill the patient.

Business ethics - paradoxically, to be ethical may be good for business as it implies treating people properly.

Meta-ethics - David Hume, who is the father of logical positivism (with the analytic/synthetic distinction of meaningfulness) is also the father of utilitarian naturalism. He seems to appear on both sides of the naturalism debate.

Conscience - neither Aquinas nor Freud argue that conscience is the voice of God. Aquinas' idea of synderesis (innate intuitive knowledge of right and wrong) is paradoxically not very different from Dawkins' argument for an altruistic gene.

Sexual ethics - to be happiest in our sexual decisions it may be best to integrate the four loves of Greek philosophy (agape meaning sacrificial love, philia meaning friendship love, storge meaning family love, and eros meaning erotic/creative love). Paradoxically just following pleasure can make us miserable.

Christian Thought H573/3

Augustine on Human Nature - seems pessimistic to argue that original sin is transmitted by male semen. Aquinas' view that we are orientated towards the good is more optimistic. Arguably the Bible suggests both.

Death and the Afterlife - connects with discussions of the soul in Philosophy of Religion and body/soul debates (monism versus dualism).

Natural Knowledge of God - Alister McGrath is rehabilitating natural theology in his recent work - arguing it is not trying to prove God's existence but instead provide an integrating 'fiduciary framework' or faith perspective on all reality.

Person of Christ - link with liberation theology's view of Jesus the radical liberator, and compare with historic statements of the Church such as the

Chalcedonian creed of 451. Why has the political role of Christ been underplayed in history (except in Latin America)?

Christian Moral Principles - are contained in both the actions of Christ (he seems to prefer outsiders and outcasts) and the teachings of Christ (such as the beatitudes of Matthew 5). But are they culturally relativised? Why is Christianity so invisible in Britain today (compared with Latin America?).

Christian Moral Action - if Christians today took Bonhoeffer's insights on costly grace more seriously arguably they would not be so invisible. Bonhoeffer is also important for his teaching on leadership - the servant-leader has arguably much to teach our age.

Pluralistic theology - Christian liberalism and universalism emerges in the Enlightenment. It's worth researching John Hick carefully on this subject - but arguably his end-product isn't Christianity.

Secularism - Charles Taylor has done most work on the subject of secularism. His conclusion that we need to form communities around the value of agape love seems to echo Joseph Fletcher.

Feminism - Mary Daly was criticised by Audrey Lourde for providing a white, middle class, privileged perspective on feminism. It's worth researching her criticisms. Daly also ran into trouble for excluding men from her classes in Boston University. Can the Catholic Church evangelise a secular age if it excludes women from the priesthood? Can the church have a prophetic role if issues of justice aren't primary?

Possible Future Questions

Past exam questions from the OCR board are in italics (copyright OCR 2018). The same question cannot be asked twice, but of course, the same theme can emerge in a differently-worded question.

Possible Exam Questions - Philosophy of Religion H573/1

Plato – the Cave/Forms

- Critically compare Plato's Form of the Good with Aristotle's Prime Mover.

- 'In their attempts to make sense of reality, Plato relies too much on rationalism and Aristotle relies too much on empirical observation'. Discuss

- Assess the claim that Plato does not value experience enough.

- 'Plato's Theory of Forms explains how we know what we know.' Discuss

Aristotle - Empiricism

- 'Aristotle successfully proves the existence of the Prime Mover.' Discuss.

- Assess Aristotle's argument for the Four Causes.

- 'Aristotle's reliance on empiricism has many weaknesses'. Discuss

- Evaluate whether Plato's rationalism is superior to Aristotle's empiricism in making sense of reality.

Soul – Mind, Body, Spirit

- Assess the claim that disembodied existence is possible.

- 'The body is separate from the soul.' Discuss

- 'The concept of the soul is best understood as a metaphor.' Discuss

- 'The mind/body distinction is a category error.' Evaluate this view.

Soul, Body, Mind, Spirit - Monism

- 'The body and soul cannot be separated.' Discuss.

- Assess whether the soul is best considered as reality or as metaphor.

- Evaluate what Aristotle meant by arguing that the soul is the form of the body.

- 'The body dies, but the soul lives forever'. Discuss

Ontological Argument

- 'Anselm's Ontological Argument proves God exists logically.' Discuss.

- Assess the claim that existence is a predicate.

- 'A priori arguments for God's existence are more persuasive than a posteriori arguments'. Discuss

- Critically evaluate the view that the ontological argument contains a number of logical fallacies which nullify the conclusion that God exists.

Cosmological Argument

- Assess the claim that the cosmological argument proves that God exists a posteriori.

- 'Hume's challenges successfully disprove the cosmological argument.' Discuss.

- 'The cosmological argument jumps to the conclusion that there is a transcendental creator without sufficient explanation'. Discuss

- 'Aquinas' first three ways provide compelling reasons to believe in God'. Discuss

Teleological Argument

- *To what extent does Hume successfully argue that observation does not prove the existence of God? (OCR June 2018)*

- 'The teleological argument proves that the universe is designed.' Discuss.

- Assess Hume's challenges of the teleological argument.

- Critically evaluate a priori against a posteriori arguments for God's existence.

- Can teleological arguments be successfully defended against the challenge of 'chance' and natural selection?

Religious Experience

- *'Corporate religious experiences are less reliable than individual religious experiences'. Discuss (OCR June 2018)*

- Assess the claim that religious experiences prove that God exists.

- 'Religious experiences are nothing more than forms of psychological neurosis.' Discuss.

- 'Personal testimony can never be reliable evidence for God's existence'. Discuss

- Critically compare corporate religious experiences with individual experiences as a basis for belief in God.

Problem of Evil

- 'There is no solution to the problem of evil and suffering.' Discuss.

- Assess the success of John Hick's argument for soul-making as a development of Irenaeus' theodicy.

- Assess which logical or evidential aspects of the problem of evil pose the greatest challenge to belief.

- Critically assess whether it is possible to defend monotheism in the face of the existence of evil.

Nature of God

- *Assess Boethius' view that divine eternity does not limit human free will. (OCR June 2018)*

- Critically assess the philosophical problems raised by believing in an omnibenevolent God.

- Evaluate the philosophical problems raised by the belief that God is eternal.

- Assess the claim that the universe shows no evidence of the existence of a benevolent God.

- Critically assess the problems for believers who say that God is omniscient.

- Boethius was successful in his argument that God rewards and punishes justly. Discuss.

- Critically assess the philosophical problems raised by belief that God is omniscient.

Classical Religious Language

- *'The best approach to understanding religious language is through the cataphatic way'. Discuss (OCR June 2018)*

- To what extent is the Via Negativa the only way to talk about God?

- Evaluate the claim that analogy can successfully be used to express the human understanding of God.

- Critically assess the views of Paul Tillich on religious language.

Religious Language – Twentieth Century Approaches

- Critically assess Wittgenstein's belief that language games allow religious statements to have meaning.

- The falsification principle presents no real challenge to religious belief. Discuss

- Critically assess the claim that religious language is meaningless.

Possible Exam Questions - Ethics H573/2

Past exam questions are in italics for reference purposes.

Natural Law

- Natural law succeeds because it takes human nature seriously. Discuss

- *'Natural Law does not present a helpful method for making moral decisions'. Discuss*

- *'Moral decisions should be based on duty, not purpose'. Assess with reference to the theory of Natural Law.*

- *'Human beings are born with the tendency to pursue morally good ends'. Evaluate in the light of teleological aspects of Natural Law.*

- Critically assess the view that natural law is the best approach to issues surrounding sexual ethics.

Kant

- *'Kantian ethics is helpful in providing practical guidelines for making moral decisions in every context'. Discuss*

- Evaluate to what extent duty can be the sole basis for a moral action.

- *'Kantian ethics is too abstract to be useful in practical ethical decision-making'. Discuss*

- 'In neglecting the role of emotions in favour of pure reason, Kantian ethics fails to give a realistic account of our human nature'. Discuss

Utilitarianism

- Evaluate the view that utilitarianism does not provide a helpful way of solving moral dilemmas.

- To what extent, if any, is Utilitarianism a useful theory for approaching moral decisions in life?

- Utilitarianism provides a helpful method of moral decision making. Discuss Already marked

- "The application of the greatest happiness principle in specific situations is not a sufficient guide to the good action". Discuss

- 'Pleasure is not quantifiable'. Discuss

- To what extent does utilitarian ethics provide a useful guide to issues surrounding business ethics?

Situation Ethics

- 'Situation ethics is too demanding as a system of ethical decision-making'. Discuss

- 'Goodness is only defined by asking - how is agape best served'. Discuss

- 'Agape is not so much a religious idea as an equivalent to saying 'I want the best for you". Discuss

- Evaluate the extent to which situation ethics is individualistic and subjective.

Applied - Euthanasia (Natural Law and Situation Ethics)

- *Assess the view that natural law is of no use with regard to the issue of euthanasia. (OCR June 2018)*

- Natural Law is superior to situation ethics in its treatment of issues surrounding euthanasia". Discuss

- 'Autonomy as an ideal is unrealistic. No-one is perfectly autonomous'. Discuss with reference to the ethical issue of euthanasia.

- 'Explain and justify the doctrine of double effect with reference to an ethical dilemma of your choice concerning euthanasia'.

- 'Sanctity of human life is the core principle of medical ethics'. Discuss

- 'There is no moral difference between actively ending a life by euthanasia and omitting to treat the patient'. Discuss

Applied – Business Ethics (Kant and Utilitarianism)

- *Kantian ethics is the best approach to Business Ethics". Discuss (OCR June 2018)*

- 'Kantian ethic of duty is superior to the utilitarian ethic of happiness in dealing with difficult business decisions'. Discuss

- Critically discuss the view that businesses have a moral duty to put their customers first. Already marked

- Critically discuss the view that businesses have a moral duty to put their customers first. Patrick King

- 'Corporate social responsibility is ethical window-dressing to cover their greed'. Discuss

- Evaluate the view that capitalism will always exploit human beings in the pursuit of profit.

- 'Globalisation widens the exploitation of human beings by reducing the need for ethically valid regulation of business behaviour". Discuss

Meta-ethics

- *'Good' is meaningful. Discuss (OCR June 2018)*

- "The meaning of the word 'good' is the defining question in the study of ethics". Discuss

- Critically consider whether ethical terms such as good, bad, right and wrong have an objective factual basis that makes them true or false.

- 'Ethical statements are merely an expression of an emotion'. Discuss
  Already marked

- Evaluate the view that ethical statements are meaningless.

- 'People know what's right or wrong by a common sense intuition'. Discuss

- Critically contrast the views of intuitionists and emotivists on the origin and meaning of ethical statements.

Conscience

- *Evaluate Aquinas' theological approach to conscience. (OCR June 2018)*

- Critically contrast the theories of conscience of Aquinas and Freud.

- 'Conscience is given by God, not formed by childhood experience'. Critically evaluate this view with reference to Freud and Aquinas.

- 'Conscience is a product of culture, environment, genetic predisposition and education'. Discuss

- 'Conscience is another word for irrational feelings of guilt'. Discuss

- 'Freud's theory of conscience has no scientific basis. It is merely hypothesis'. Discuss

- 'Guilt feelings are induced by social relationships as a method of control'. Discuss

- Is Conscience linked to or separate from reason and the unconscious mind?

Sexual Behaviour

- 'In terms of sexual ethical decisions, all you need to do is apply your conscience'. Discuss

- 'Religion is irrelevant in deciding issues surrounding sexual behaviour'. Discuss

- Critically evaluate the view that the ethics of sexual behaviour should be entirely private and personal.

- 'Because sexual conduct affects others, it should be subject to legislation'. Discuss

- 'Normative theories are useful in what they might say about sexual ethics'. Discuss

Possible Exam Questions – Christian Thought
H573/3

Past exam questions are in italics for reference purposes.

Augustine

- Assess the view that Augustine's teaching on human nature is too pessimistic

- Critically assess the view that Christian teaching on human nature can only make sense if the Fall did actually happen

- 'Augustine's teaching on human nature is more harmful than helpful'. Discuss.

- How convincing is Augustine's teaching about the Fall and Original Sin?

- Critically assess Augustine's analysis of human sexual nature.

Death and the Afterlife

- To what extent can belief in the existence of purgatory be justified?

- 'Heaven is not a place but a state of mind.' Discuss.

- 'Without the reward of Heaven Christians would not behave well.' Discuss

- To what extent is the Parable of the Sheep and the Goats in Matthew 25 only about Heaven and Hell?

- Assess the view that there is no last judgement; each person is judged by God at the moment of their death.

- 'Purgatory is the most important Christian teaching about the afterlife.' Discuss.

Knowledge of God

- Discuss critically the view that Christians can discover truths about God using human reason.

- 'Faith is all that is necessary to gain knowledge of God.' Discuss.

- 'God can be known because the world is so well designed.' Discuss.

- Critically assess the view that the Bible is the only way of knowing God.

- 'Everyone has an innate knowledge of God's existence.' Discuss.

- To what extent is faith in God rational?

Person of Christ

- *'To what extent was Jesus merely a political liberator?' (OCR June 2018)*

- 'There is no evidence to suggest that Jesus thought of himself as divine.' Discuss.

- To what extent can Jesus be regarded as no more than a teacher of wisdom?

- 'Jesus' role was just to liberate the poor and weak against oppression.' Discuss.

- Assess the view that the miracles prove Jesus was the Son of God.

- 'Jesus Christ is not unique.' Discuss.

- To what extent was Jesus just a teacher of morality?

Christian Moral Principles

- How fair is the claim that there is nothing distinctive about Christian ethics?

- 'The Bible is all that is needed as a moral guide for Christian behaviour.' Discuss.

- 'The Church should decide what is morally good.' Discuss.

- Assess the view that the Bible is a comprehensive moral guide for Christians.

- To what extent do Christians actually disagree about what Christian ethics are?

- To what extent should Jesus be considered only as a teacher of wisdom?

- Evaluate the extent to which Jesus may be considered as the unique Son of God.

- 'There are many Christs, but one God'. Discuss

Christian Moral Action

- *Bonhoeffer's theology is still relevant today". Discuss (OCR June 2018)*

- 'Using the will of God as a guide for moral behaviour is impractical, as in most circumstances it is impossible to know what god wants us to do.' Discuss.

- To what extent, if at all, does the theology of Bonhoeffer have relevance for Christians today?

- 'Bonhoeffer's most important teaching is on leadership.' Discuss.

- 'Christian ethics means being obedient to god's will.' Discuss.

- To what extent was Bonhoeffer's religious community at Finkenwalde successful?

Pluralism – Secular

- To what extent should Christians seek to convert others to Christianity at every opportunity?

- 'Inter-faith dialogue is of little practical use.' Discuss.

- To what extent does scriptural reasoning relativise religious beliefs?

- 'Converting people of no faith should be equally important to a Christian as converting people of a non-Christian faith.' Discuss.

Pluralism - Theological

- 'A theologically pluralist approach significantly undermines the central doctrines of Christianity.' Discuss.

- To what extent can non-Christians who live morally good lives and genuinely seek God be considered to be 'anonymous Christians'?

- Critically assess the view that only Christianity offers the means of salvation

- 'Christianity is one of many ways to salvation.' Discuss.

Secularism – Christianity Effects

- *'Secularism does not pose a threat to Christianity'. Discuss (OCR June 2018)*

- 'Christianity has a negative impact on society.' Discuss.

- To what extent are Christian values more than just basic human values?

- 'Christianity should play no part in public life.' Discuss.

- Critically assess the claims that God is an illusion and the result of wish fulfilment.

Liberation Theology

- To what extent should Christianity engage with atheist secular ideologies?

- 'Liberation theology has not engaged with Marxism fully enough.' Discuss.

- Critically assess the claim that Christianity has tackled social issues more effectively than Marxism.

- Critically assess the relationship of liberation theology and Marx with particular reference to liberation theology's use of Marx to analyse social sin.

Gender & Society

- *Assess the view that Mary Daly's feminism proves Christianity is sexist. (OCR June 2018)*

- Christians should resist current secular views of gender" Discuss

- Evaluate the view that secular views of gender equality have undermined Christian gender roles

- 'Motherhood liberates rather than restricts'. Discuss

- Critically evaluate the view that idea of family is entirely culturally determined.

- 'Christianity follows where culture leads'. Discuss

Gender & Theology

- 'A male saviour cannot save'. Discuss with reference to the theologies of Rosemary Ruether and Mary Daly.

- 'If God is male the male is God'. Discuss

- Critically contrast the theologies of Ruether and Daly.

- 'The Church is irrevocably patriarchal'. Discuss

- 'God is genderless, and so the idea of the Father-God is idolatry'. Discuss

161

- 'Only a spirituality of women can save the planet from environmental degradation and war'. Discuss

Analytical Words and Phrases

These are the kinds of words and phrases that give an empirical test whether you are writing analytically (sequencing ideas). Try using some of them and weaving together analysis and evaluation.

1. Producing reasons (justifying)

because

for this reason

this is supported by

this argument is based on

this establishes that

2. Probing deeper (underlying)

this assumes

underlying this view

this worldview suggests

this implies

from an X perspective

3. Adding something (extending)

furthermore

finally

as a result

consequently

it follows that

moreover

also

4. Placing a counter-point (contrasting)

however

on the other hand

in contrast

this contradicts

maybe (with hesitation)

perhaps (with hesitation)

although

but

5. Concluding

therefore

in short

in conclusion

to sum up

I have argued

it has been established, therefore

the preceding analysis suggests

Summary of Examiner's Comments 2018

1. Students struggled with timing. So practise writing for 40 minutes.

2. Make links across the three papers (synoptic links).

3. Make sure you balance your essay between AO1 and AO2 criteria.

4. Do your own research and don't just quote the textbook.

5. Use your own examples - make sure they're integrated to the title.

6. The opening paragraph shouldn't try to say everything.

7. Answer the question in front of you, not your prepared learnt answer.

8. Be selective in your use of knowledge, but generous in justifying it.

9. Plan your essay before you start to write.

10. Length of essay is not a requirement or a guarantee of Level 6.

You can download the full examiners' reports by asking your teacher for your centre number and then going to the OCR website. It's a good idea to try past questions with the examiners' comments in front of you and see if you can hit level 6. The level of detail they provide on the kind of knowledge and analysis expected is considerable. Then why not try some of the harder possible future questions in each topic area (see my list)? Remember to try to analyse and pre-prepare the underlying issues in each topic. Then whatever the question, you will be well-prepared.

Glossary of Key Technical Terms

Here are definitions of every technical term mentioned in the OCR specification H573/1/2/3 and a few which perhaps should have been in, which I think you should also know about.

a posteriori - means 'after experience', or 'from observation'. A posteriori arguments include the teleological argument, and the ethical theory of natural law, which derives goodness from observed rational tendencies God has designed into us.

a priori - means 'before experience". A priori arguments proceed by logical deduction, for example the ontological argument for God's existence, or Kant's theory of ethics.

absolutism - 'absolute' means one of three things - a theory is universal (applies to everyone) or that a principle is non-negotiable (unchanging) or that it is objective - tested empirically so beyond dispute.

act utilitarianism - the utility of an act is its ability to maximise happiness and minimise pain - tested by applying the greatest happiness principle to likely consequences of a single action.

agape - one of the four loves of Greek ethics, meaning unconditional commitment to friend and stranger, as in Jesus' saying 'greater agape has no-one than this, that a person lay down his life for his friends" (John 15:13). It is both the foundation principle of situation ethics, and a vital issue in Christian moral principles (Christian Thought).

analogy of attribution - Aquinas' view that you can say God is like blazing sun (attribute of purity and light). But it's an analogy because there isn't a precise one for one likeness between God and the attribute of light. As God is the cause of all good things, God's attributes are simply on a higher level to our own. Hick gave examples of 'upwards' analogy of attribution, such as speaking of a dog's faithfulness as analogical to the faithfulness of God.

analytic - statements true by definition eg 'all bachelors are unmarried' and established a priori. Evidence is not required to establish the truthfulness of analytic statements..

anaphatic (or apophatic) way - a philosophical approach to theology which asserts that no finite concepts or attributes can be adequately used of God, but only negative terms, such as immortal, immutable or invisible. Apophasis means 'denial, negation' and so 'apophatic' is another word for anaphatic.

analogy of proper proportion - A plant has a life, a human has life, God has life - there is a proportionate relationship between each life mentioned in the list, with God's being the greatest and the plants being on a proportionately lower level.

attributes - (divine) qualities of God's character such as omnibenevolence, omnipotence and omniscience. Notice these can be expressed positively as in the via positiva or negatively as in the via negativa (God is immortal, so not mortal, invisible, so not visible).

categorical imperative - A term Kant employs to express an unconditional, absolute maxim or command - an imperative like 'never lie!'

category error - applying a category from one form of life to another which it cannot refer to - such as 'what colour is the wind?" The wind never has a colour.

cognitive approaches to language - an imposition on the debate on religious and ethical language from the Enlightenment concern for verification and 'meaningfulness' - cognitive approaches examine the truth value of statements according to their verifiability (testability by experience). So 'examination of the truth-aptness of statements'.

conscientia - Aquinas' one of two words for conscience, meaning 'reason making right decisions', he other being 'synderesis', for example, judging what to do in natural law theory when two goods conflict and we need to judge how to apply the principle of double effect means applying the judgement of reason.

corporate social responsibility - a theory developed by Edward Freeman which states that corporations should take responsibility for the consequences of their actions for all stakeholders and for the environment, and not just shareholders.

cosmological - to do with first causes - the cosmological argument is concerned to establish God as first cause of everything (as first muted by Aristotle's prime mover).

divine law - one of the four laws of natural law ethics, sees the inaccessible eternal law revealed to us in two ways by God - by divine law (the Bible) and natural law (morality). Echoes here of Plato's Forms of the good and Kant's noumenal (inaccessible) realm of reality.

efficient cause - one of Aristotle's four causes which implies the process by which something comes into being - eg the sculptor forms the clay to make his art.

ego - one of Freud's three classifications of the human psyche, the ego is the reality principle which forms as we realise how to present ourselves to the public world, even with the contradictions and conflicts within us.

election - the belief that God, with no regard to the will of man, made an eternal choice of certain persons to have eternal life and some to eternal damnation and that number is so fixed that it cannot be changed. Popular view in Calvinism.

emotivism - a theory of ethical language developed by AJ Ayer from the logical positivists of the Vienna Circle, which concludes that all ethical statements are simply expressions of emotion and have no factual (cognitive, truth-apt) content.

empiricism - the view that the meaningfulness and truth conditions of experience are required to test our knowledge of reality. Their views affect both issues of language and of testability, but as the empiricist Hume concedes there is a problem in induction - we cannot finally prove the sun will rise tomorrow.

eternal law - one fo the four laws of Aquinas' natural law which refers to the inaccessible mind and purposeful design of God, whose blueprint is only partially revealed to us.

exclusivism - a view in the debate about theological pluralism which states that Jesus is the only 'way, the truth and the life' as in John 14:6.

extramarital sex - sexual relations outside marriage between at least one married person and another (irrespective of gender).

fall - the Fall of humankind in Genesis 3 occurred when Eve disobeyed God by taking the fruit from the tree of knowledge and giving it to Adam, who disobeys by eating it. In consequence, they are expelled from Eden, Eve gets pain in childbirth and Adam finds weeds growing in the garden as God's curse - also Adam 'has dominion' over Eve and she 'desires him' - Augustine sees this as the moment lust (cupiditas) enters the world.

fallacy - a mistake in deductive logic when one thing doesn't follow from another. In the naturalistic fallacy (meta-ethics) the fallacy is that we move from is statements to ought statements without supplying an answer to the question - this may be pleasurable, but what exactly makes it good?

falsificationism - conditions by which a proposition may be considered false, for example, the proposition 'the sun will rise tomorrow' can be falsified because the sun may not rise tomorrow.

five ways - the five proofs in Aquinas for the existence of God which include - the unmoved mover, the first cause, the argument from necessity (contingency), the argument from degree, and the argument from ends (the teleological argument). All these are forms of cosmological argument. Richard Dawkins criticisms of Aquinas' argument has been challenged by Keith ward and Alister McGrath.

formal cause - the concept in the mind of the sculptor before he takes the clay (material cause), sculpts (efficient cause) and produces a work of art (final cause). the formal cause of the existence of the universe is part of God's eternal law in natural law ethics.

formula of kingdom of ends - Kant's formal principe, that defines goodness, that we should so act as to imagine ourselves a lawmaker in a kingdom of ends, with the consistent rules that would follow.

formula of law of nature (law) - Kant's formula that we should act according to a maxim which can be willed as a universal law for the whole fo humanity.

formula of the end in itself (ends) - Kant's formula, often misquoted, that we should treat people not simply as a means to an end, but always also as an end in themselves. He never said as Fletcher states - don't treat people as means, but only as ends.

globalisation - the process of opening up global markets and global culture so that people trade, interchange and share products, views, and values freely and without restrictions.

grace - God's generous gifts to humanity of love, sustaining power, and life itself. Jesus is described as 'full of grace and truth' (John 1:14). Closely linked to the character of God int he Old Testament of hesed (Hebrew - steadfast love) and emeth (Hebrew - truth or faithfulness).

hedonic calculus - Bentham's way of calculating the balance of pleasure over pain in an action by seven criteria - things such as intensity, extent and duration of the pleasure.

hypothetical imperative - a command with an 'if' in it - if you are faced with an axe murderer asking after your friend, you should lie (a famous Kantian example). Kant felt morality was based on categorical absolutes, not conditional statements with an 'if' making them relative to circumstances.

id - Freud's term for the part of the psyche which follows the pleasure principle of satisfying needs and desires, typified by the screaming baby.

inclusivism - a term in religious pluralism which means that all ways (religions) lead to God, and no one path excludes others. Hick's universal pluralism is an example.

innate - means 'born with' and so in natural law ethics we are all born with a tendency to do good and avoid evil, a kind of inbuilt knowledge Aquinas called synderesis.

intuitionism - a theory of goodness that holds that we know right and wrong by intuition, a kind of inbuilt perception. GE Moore argues that good is an indefinable, non-reducible, simple property of an action which we just recognise like the colour yellow.

invincible ignorance - ignorance of sin and morality which Aquinas believes gives us an excuse, for example, because we have never heard of Jesus or the Bible.

limited election - the argument that only certain people will be saved - either those predestined (Calvin) or those who have repented and chosen to believe (general Protestant view)

material cause - the stuff something is made of, such as clay in a sculpture.

materialism - a Marxist idea that human beings have been reduced to an object which is in fundamental conflict with other objects, particularly the capitalist against the worker where both are 'objectified'. Also refers more generally to a human desire and obsession to get wealth.

messiah - the 'anointed one', and the hope of Israel that one day 'a son is born, a son is given who shall be called wonderful counsellor, Mighty God, Prince of Peace'. In the Person of Christ section of Christian Thought, the debate about whether Jesus thought himself the special one (Messiah) in a divine sense and what the title 'Son of God' actually meant.

meta-ethics - 'beyond ethics' so the language and meaning of ethical terms, and questions of the foundation of ethics, whether it is naturalistic (something in the world) or non-naturalistic.

metaphysics - beyond physics and so that which is not observable/ measurable by science, such as truth, beauty and love (includes God, of course).

mystical experience - experience that cannot be explained by science or medicine, such as the visions of St Teresa of Avila, or Paul's meeting Christ on the road to Damascus in Acts.

natural knowledge - knowledge that can be gained from observing nature. The teleological argument, that God has designed patterns into nature, is an inference from natural knowledge.

natural law - a theory of ethics originating from Aristotle and developed by Aquinas, that human beings have a true rational purpose designed into them, observable a posteriori by the goals we by our natures pursue. The 'unofficial moral theology of the Catholic Church' (Singer).

natural religion - religion based on reason rather than divine revelation, especially deism which became popular during the Enlightenment.

naturalism - a debate in meta-ethics about the foundation of ethics, whether it exists in the natural world, or as part of our experience (such as pleasure and pain) or whether it's source is a priori (so non-natural, as Kant agues).

nature of attributes of God - attributes of God typically include his omniscience, omnipotence and omnibenevolence (which are linked to his powers) or faithfulness, steadfast-love and generosity (related to his moral character and holiness).

non-cognitive approaches to language - non-cognitive means 'not truth-apt' ie not verifiable by reference to something else such as observation or experience.

normative means of salvation - the ways by which God saves us, where 'normative' means 'those defined as true and accepted'. In Christianity the normative means of salvation is the cross of Christ, by which he paid the price as a ransom for sin (Mark 10:45).

omnibenevolence - all-loving attribute of God

omnipotence - all-powerful attribute of God

omniscience - all-knowing attribute of God

ontological - means 'of the essence' as in the ontological argument for the existence of God which derives from his essence as ever-existing and perfect.

original sin - sin coming from the choice of Adam and Eve in the Garden to disobey God and eat the fruit of the tree of knowledge. Augustine believed this original sin was transmitted ever-after by the male semen. It's a debate in Knowledge of God (Christian Thought) how much we can 'see' God ourselves in nature, and how much original sin permanently blinds us.

personalism - one of the working principles of Situation ethics, meaning 'related to the effect on the individual'. Fletcher argues ethics should be related to individual needs and desires, not imposed as law.

pluralism - means 'many views of truth and goodness'.

positivism - has two meanings, rather different. Fletcher cites positivism as a working principle of situation ethics, meaning 'received by faith and then lived by'. Whereas in logical positivism in meta-ethics and religious language it means 'provable by a principle of verification'.

postulates - things put forward as self-evident, as assumptions, as in Kant's ethical theory which postulates God, immortality and freedom.

pragmatism - one of Fletcher's four working principles in situation ethics, meaning 'practical, based on a real case-by-case approach to ethics'.

predicate - 'existence is not a predicate' said Kant of the ontological argument. "God exists" appears to attribute a property, existence, to a subject, God. 'Exists' here is the predicate describing something about God but seems to assume what it is describing (that God exists).

primary precept - the five precepts mentioned by Aquinas as the natural rational goals of human beings (preserve life, order society, worship God, educate and reproduce).

prime mover - an Aristotelean idea that something (God) put the world and cosmos into existence. Became associated with Deism in the eighteenth century as God gets progressively distanced from his creation.

purgatory - a state of being between death and heaven when the soul is purified (or purged) of sin.

ratio - the reason by which we work out the eternal law of God evidenced in experience and by observation. Synderesis in contrast, in natural law ethics, is intuitive reason.

rationalism - a principle of the Enlightenment which has as its motto 'dare to reason' and which exalts reason over metaphysics, and so closely linked to scepticism and secularism (Christian Thought specification). In meta-ethics and religious language debates, influences of rationalists like David Hume cause people to doubt the meaningfulness of religious language.

relativism - means one of three things, relative to consequences, subjective (up to me) or particular to culture (as in 'cultural relativism').

repentance - Greek 'metanoia' means to change direction by renouncing one way and actively embracing another. The first call of Jesus in Mark's gospel is 'repent, for the Kingdom of Heaven is at hand'. In Liberation Theology it means taking up the cause of justice and revolution and overturning social evils.

rule utilitarianism - a theory of ethics normally attributed to JS Mill which argues that maximising happiness involves the recognition of certain (non-absolute) social rules which past experience confirms as good.

salvation - the process of being saved by the activity (grace) of God.

sanctity of life - the specialness and uniqueness of human life based either on the will of God in creating us and sustaining us, or some rational principle as in Kantian ethics, where it is seen as inconsistent to will your own death..

secondary precept - applications by human reason of primary precepts (primary goods of natural law) to specific circumstances.

secularism - the progressive separation of private religion and public human affairs, and the evacuation of metaphysics from the realm of public debate.

sinful - sin is lawlessness, and falling short, and disobeying God.

son of god - title given to Jesus which might mean 'special anointed one' or possibly just 'the human one'.

soul - part of a human being that is metaphysical and separate from the body. Dualism is the belief we have a body and a soul and the soul goes on to eternal existence after death as a different substance. Monism argues body and soul are one.

stakeholders - all those who have an interest in the activities of a corporation, includes shareholders, employees, the local community, suppliers, the Government etc.

substance dualism - states that two sorts of substances exist: the mental and the physical. Substance dualism is a fundamentally ontological position: it states that the mental and the physical are separate substances with independent existence.

summum bonum - the greatest good, a term used in ethics (eg Kant) for the ultimate goal or result of good actions.

superego -that part of the Freudian psyche which mediates between right and wrong and resolves conflicts between ego and id.

synderesis - a term in natural law ethics meaning we have natural innate disposition to 'do good and avid evil'. Aquinas also calls it the 'intuitive knowledge of first principles', which we normally refer to as the five primary precepts.

synthetic - statements are true by experience and so may be verified a posteriori. Analytic/synthetic distinction originates with David Hume, and is developed by Logical Positivists.

teleological - telos means end or purpose. So a teleological argument looks at the purpose in patterns of design in the world, as in Paley's watchmaker analogy. Teleological ethics is the ethics of purpose - as in utilitarian ethics (happiness) or situation ethics (love).

teleology - the study of purpose in nature or in ethics.

telos - Greek for purpose or end (goal)

The Forms - Plato's word for the reality behind and beyond reality which we only see as shadows in a cave. The Theory of Forms is Plato's answer to the problem "how one unchanging reality or essential being can appear in so many changing phenomena."

theodicies- rational philosophies which provide an explanation for the presence of evil in the face of the providence and goodness of God.

universalist belief - the belief that all people everywhere will eventually be saved, irrespective of their faith position.

utility - means 'usefulness' as in utilitarianism which states that we can make a practical calculation of happiness of the greatest number, a view made popular by Jeremy Bentham and John Stuart Mill (19th century).

verificationism - a philosophical theory that holds that for propositions to meaningful they must be susceptible to rational proof by observation.

via negativa (anaphatic way) - a philosophical approach to theology which asserts that no finite concepts or attributes can be adequately used of God, but only negative terms, such as immortal, invisible. Apophasis means 'denial, negation' and so 'apophatic' is another word for anaphatic.

via positiva (cataphatic way) - uses "positive" terminology to describe or refer to the divine – specifically, God – i.e. terminology that describes or refers to what the divine is believed to be.

vincible ignorance - ignorance that a person could remove by applying reasonable diligence in the given set of circumstances, so blameworthy ignorance, echoing Paul in Romans 2, 'the Gentiles are without excuse' because we all have the moral law written on our hearts.

whistle-blowing - the practice in business ethics whereby an employee reveals malpractice, now protected as a right in UK law.

working principles - the four principles in situation ethics which define how agape love applies in practice: personalism, positivism, pragmatism and relativism.

About the Author

Peter Baron is a leading teacher and teacher-trainer, with many years experience helping his students gain top grades. He studied PPE at New College Oxford, then Hermeneutics at Newcastle University. He qualified as an Economics teacher in 1982, and from 2006-12 taught ethics at Wells Cathedral School in Somerset. He currently works as a freelance writer, speaker, trainer and educational consultant, and is author of revision guides and coursebooks on ethics.

In 2007 he set up a philosophy and ethics community dedicated to enlarging the teaching of philosophy in schools by applying the theory of multiple intelligences to the analysis of philosophical and ethical problems. So far over 600 schools have joined the community and over 30,000 individuals use his website every month.

To join the community please register your interest by filling in your details on the form on the website. We welcome contributions and suggestions so that our community continues to flourish and expand.

www.peped.org

Printed in Great Britain
by Amazon